MEXICAN

healthy ——— a favorite cuisine

HERMES HOUSE

MEXICAN

ways with a favorite cuisine

JANE MILTON

Publisher: Joanna Lorenz
Executive Editor: Linda Fraser
Senior Editor: Joanne Rippin
Consultant Editor: Jenni Fleetwood
Designer:Nigel Partridge
Photography: Simon Smith (recipes) and Janine Hosegood (reference)
Food for Photography: Caroline Barty (recipes) and Annabel Ford (reference)

Front cover shows Tacos with shredded beef. For recipe see page 146.
Previously published as *The Practical Encyclopedia of Mexican Cooking*

1 3 5 7 9 10 8 6 4 2

ACKNOWLEDGEMENTS

Thanks to my Mum for typing my recipes and to Dad for proof reading everything - I would never have made my deadlines without your help. Thanks too to Tom Estes of Cafe Pacifico, for sharing his knowledge of tequila and much more, and for his enthusiasm for this project.

The publishers would to thank South American Pictures for the use of their photographs in the book: 8bl, tr; 9tl, br; 10t; 11tl, br; 12tl, tr, bl; 13tl, m, br; 14tr, ml, bl; 15tl, br; 16tr, bl; 17tl, br; 18tr, mr, bl; 19tr, ml, bl.

NOTES

For all recipes, quantities are given in both metric and imperial measures and, where appropriate, measures are also given in standard cups and spoons, Follow one set, but not a mixture, because they are not interchangable.

Standard spoon and cup measures are level.

1 tsp = 5ml, 1tbsp = 15ml, 1 cup = 250ml/8fl oz

Australian standard tablespoons are 20ml, Australian readers should use 3 tsp in place of 1tbsp for measuring small quantities of gelatine, cornflour, salt etc.

Medium eggs are used unless otherwise stated.

CONTENTS

INTRODUCTION

Mexican food mirrors the [...]y — it is colorful, rich, stimulating and festive. From the wild the sultry heat of the south, this vast country offers the food lo[...]s. The waters of the Gulf of Mexico and the Pacific Ocean teem[...]e sub-tropical regions that adjoin them yield abundant fruit, incl[...] papayas. From the gardens of the high plateau come wonderful [...]orth is cattle country. Chiles of every shape, color and size are [...]avors ranging from subtle to strident, [...] providing the sig[...] world's most exciting cuisines.

HISTORY OF COOKING IN MEXICO

Food is a very important aspect of the Mexican way of life. Producing and purchasing the raw materials, preparing food and eating it account for a large part of each day, and wonderful dishes are created to mark special occasions and celebrations.

Some Historical Influences on the Mexican Diet

In pre-Columbian Mexico there was already an established pattern of agriculture. Foods such as corn, beans, chiles and bell peppers were widely cultivated, along with avocados, tomatoes, sweet potatoes, guavas and pineapples. Vegetables such as *jicama, chayote* and *sapote* were also grown.

During the Mayan era, the priests, who were the ruling class, allocated land for the growing of crops. They also arranged for the storage of seed and the distribution of surplus food. The warlike Aztecs, who came to power in the 15th century, were less inclined to share. Their rulers appropriated food for themselves, including chocolate, which was made into a frothy drink believed to be an aphrodisiac.

The Aztecs inherited a rich culinary tradition. The central market in Tenochtitlan was famous for its fabulous array of foods, and it is reported that

Montezuma often required of his servants that they prepare more than two dozen dishes daily for his delectation. The emperor would then stroll among the groaning tables, discussing the ingredients with his chefs, before making his selection. During the subsequent meal, young women, chosen for their beauty, would bring him hot tortillas and gold cups filled with frothy chocolate.

Columbus Comes to Mexico

When the Spaniards first arrived in Mexico in 1492, they had few cooks with them, and so local people were hired to prepare food. Dishes made with corn, chiles, beans, tomatoes and chocolate were prepared, and the Spaniards became particularly fond of chiles, chocolate and vanilla. With the Spanish came livestock, which was warmly welcomed. Until this time, the native turkeys and the occasional wild boar were the only source of meat.

The introduction of the domestic pig was significant not merely for its meat, but also for the lard, which was used for frying and became a staple ingredient in Mexican kitchens. Frying had not been possible before, due to the absence of

Above: Corn cultivation in Mexico's pre-Columbian era. Mural by Diego Rivera.

animal fats and oils. The Spaniards began to adapt their own recipes to the local ingredients, and the local people in turn adapted their cooking to include meat, which had been such a rarity in the past. The fusion began.

In 1519 the Spanish adventurer Hernando Cortés landed near the site of present day Veracruz. Within three years he had conquered Mexico, and the country was ruled as a viceroyalty of Spain for the next three hundred years. Cortés portrayed himself as the liberator of the tribes oppressed by the Aztecs and used his fanatical missionary zeal to justify his own exploitation of the Mexicans. Monks and nuns were sent from Spain to convert the pagan Mexicans to Catholicism. When they reached the New World, these religious missionaries had more than missals in their luggage; they also brought seeds, and soon citrus fruit, wheat, rice and onions augmented the supplies that served the Mexican kitchen.

Texas is Lost to the United States

Mexican independence from Spain was finally gained in 1821, after a lengthy war. Three years later, on the death of General Iturbide, a new republic was established. At that time Mexico possessed large tracts of land in what is

Below: A modern mural by Diego Rivera showing pre-Columbian corn sellers.

now the United States, including Texas. In 1836 Texas formed an independent republic, joining the United States some nine years later. This triggered the Mexican Civil War, as a result of which Mexico ceded to the United States all territories north of the Rio Grande. From a culinary perspective, this is significant, as it helps to explain the historic links between Mexico and the "Lone Star" State, and the origin of the Tex-Mex style of cooking. It also accounts for the popularity of the Mexican style of cooking in California and New Mexico.

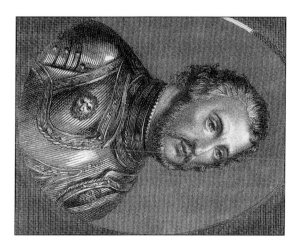

Above: Hernando Cortés, the Spanish conqueror of Mexico.

French Occupation of Mexico

The Civil War proved costly in financial terms, and put the country greatly in debt to France, England and Spain. When they could no longer repay the debt to France, that country seized the opportunity to take control of Mexico. Austrian-born Maximilian Hapsburg, a relative of Napoleon, was put in charge of the French occupation. The French met with considerable resistance and the *Cinco de Mayo* (May 5th) holiday commemorates a famous Mexican victory over their forces. However, the success was short-lived, and France installed Maximilian as the Emperor of Mexico in 1864. The French occupa[tion] lasted only three years, but left a las[ting]

ads and
cooking is
Maximilian's
experienced
but since
le.

ten described
ans "a mixture"
d only to the
es and Spanish
s many culinary
its borders,
of brewing by
rmans also
w called queso
town in northern
rs lived. The
t-and-sour

onal dress
he Mestizos.

dishes in the Mexican cuisine reflects an Asian influence, as does the Mexican classification of foods as "hot" or "cold." This has nothing to do with the temperature at which these foods are served, but relates instead to the effect they have on the body. "Hot" foods are considered to be easily digested and warming, whereas foods designated as "cold" are considered difficult to digest and likely to lower body heat. Examples of hot foods are coffee, honey and rice, while fish, limes and boiled eggs are all regarded as cold. A proper balance between hot and cold foods is believed to be vital for good health.

Mexican cuisine is sure to continue to evolve, adapt and embrace foreign influences. It is also likely to become more homogenous, as regional recipes are absorbed in the national repertoire. Like its language, the food and eating habits of a country are never static.

REGIONAL COOKING IN MEXICO

Mexico has not one single cuisine, but many. It is a vast country, the third largest in Latin America, with a wide diversity of landscapes, from snow-capped mountains to citrus groves, and a distinct range of climatic zones. These geographical factors have helped to shape a variety of different styles of cooking within the same country. The extremely mountainous nature of the landscape led, in the days before the Spanish Conquest, to the development of a large number of isolated and completely distinct Indian communities, each with its own style of cooking. When the Spanish invaded, they certainly had a considerable impact on the cuisine in the areas where they were most active, but parts of the country remained impervious to their influence, and the people there continued to cook in much the same

Above: Bananas and mangoes on sale in a street market in Chihuahua.

way as their parents and grandparents had done before them.

Even today, when tourism has introduced new ingredients and ideas, there remain pockets of Mexico where contact with the outside world is limited, and where old dishes, some of which hark back to Aztec times, are preserved.

The altitude, rather than the latitude, determines the climate in Mexico. The coastal region below 3000 feet is *tierra caliente*—the hot zone. Here the climate is sub-tropical, and mangoes, pineapples and avocados flourish. Next comes *tierra templada*, the temperate zone, which rises to 6000 feet.

Culinary Regions

Even in present-day Mexico, regional foods are still very important. This is due in some measure to the different climates, which mean certain things cannot grow in every area, or to favorable geographic locations: in Vera Cruz, a coastal area, fish dishes are prevalent. In the coming years this is likely to change as improved transportation allows products from the different regions to be transported more easily and quickly between areas.

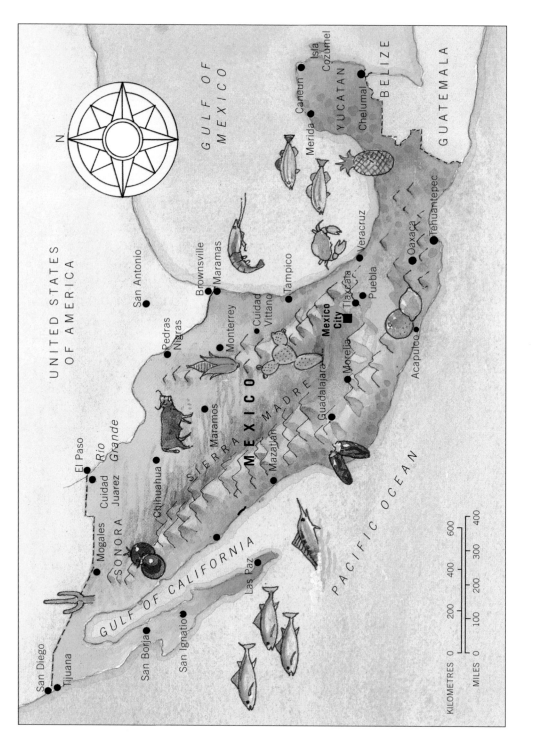

Baja California is a peninsula in the northwestern corner of the country, bordering the Pacific and the Gulf of California. It is the oldest continuously producing wine-making region of Mexico. In recent years the region's wines, particularly the whites, have won international acclaim.

The Coastal Regions

The northern Pacific coast has some magnificent beaches. The sea is well stocked with fish, especially bass, tuna and swordfish. *Ceviche*, that delicious dish made of raw fish "cooked" by the action of lime juice, is very popular in the region. It is often made from shrimp or other local shellfish.

This area generally has good soil, and grains of various types are widely cultivated, as well as chiles and other vegetables. So famous are the tomatoes produced in this region that the state basketball team is called *Tomateros* (the tomato growers). There are a number of coconut plantations along the coast, and dishes such as coconut soup are popular. Further south is the state of Jalisco, the home of tequila. Red snapper are caught on this part of the coast and cooked over open fires.

Below: Maguey, growing here in the Oaxaca valley, is used in tequila.

Above: Cooking tortillas in a Mexican street-cafe.

Caldiddo and carne seca.

ir
th
iting the
ally treating it
v
er.
re as popular
sewhere. A
harros or
, cooked with
rbs and spices
loved is the
d in homes

strial heart of
loys a large
ation, and this
rrachos, a dish
s. The soft flour
; because this is
o where wheat is
ble parcels of
wrapped in wheat
cal of this region.

Many familiar vegetables and fruits are grown in Mexico, including green beans, bell peppers, tomatoes, cabbages, cauliflowers, onions, eggplant and zucchini. At the greatest altitude lies the cold zone (*tierra fría*).

These areas of Mexico are all very different from each other, and when it is considered that the rainfall varies from as little as 2 inches a year in the northwest to over 120 inches in parts of the southwest, it is easy to comprehend how so many diverse styles of cooking came to evolve. Better infrastructure may mean that the regionality of the cuisine will be eroded in time, but at the moment each region has a strong individual identity.

The North

The northern area of Mexico, stretching from Sonora, near the Gulf of California to Monterrey in Nuevo León, has some striking contrasts. The mountain areas are sparsely populated, and life here very tough. Sonora and Chihuahua are the cattle rearing parts of Mexico. Good grazing encouraged the Spanish to establish herds of their hardy longhorns here, and specialties of the region

Above: Prickly pear cactus growing at Santa Bulalia.

Down the coast is Acapulco, a very cosmopolitan city with Latin, Asian and indigenous Indian influences. The cuisine of this area—Oaxaca—has strong Spanish influences, but is also home to some of the most traditional Mexican dishes, such as the *moles*—gloriously rich meat stews that incorporate nuts and chocolate. This is orange country, too, and citrus fruit features strongly in the recipes of the region. *Asadero*, a supple cheese similar to the Italian cheese *Provolone*, originated in Oaxaca.

Chiapas, the southernmost state bordering Guatemala, exhibits some influences from that country. Chiles are commonly served alongside dishes, as accompaniments, rather than as integral ingredients.

The eastern seaboard, lapped by the Gulf Caribbean Sea, is known as the Gulf Coast. The climate here is tropical, and this is reflected in the food. Bananas, vanilla, avocados, coffee and coconuts grow on the coast, mangoes and pineapples in the south, and to the north are orchards of apples and pears. The Gulf Coast has abundant fish stocks. The southern state of Tabasco, on the isthmus of Tehuantepec, is

Below: A palm tree in Chetumal with coconuts ready for harvesting.

particularly famous for its fish. The catch includes sea bass, striped bass, crabs, lobsters and shrimp. The port of Veracruz has a famous fish market, with red snapper the local specialty. The cuisine in this area is rich, and many of the towns have lent their names to dishes or ingredients.

In this part of Mexico, *tamales* (little filled parcels) are rolled in banana leaves, rather than the corn husks that are used elsewhere. Another local specialty is *jicama*, a crisp vegetable, which is served raw with a sprinkling of lime juice and ground chiles.

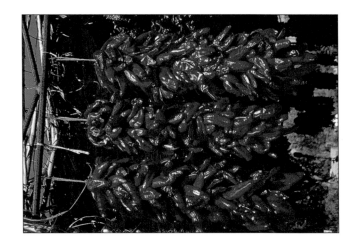

Above: Strings of chiles drying in the sun on the Pacific coast of Mexico.

Inland is the colonial town of Guadalajara, famous for *pozole*, a pork stew thickened with hominy—yellow or white corn which has been dried and has had the husk and germ removed, and which has been eaten by the Indians in Mexico for centuries. Another specialty is *birria*, a stew made from lamb or kid.

The Bajio, Central Mexico and Mexico City

To the north of Mexico City is the Bajio, a fertile area bordered by mountains. This is sometimes referred to as Colonial Mexico, and many of the local specialties are distinctly Spanish in origin, such as stuffed tongues and rich beef stews. Traditional Mexican foods are to be found here too, especially *nopales* (cactus paddles) and prickly pears (cactus fruit). *Pulque*—the drink made from the juice of the agave (or century) plant—is popular in this area. Pork is the favourite meat, often served as *Carnitas*. These are pieces of pork that are cooked in lard flavored with orange, until the outside of each piece is crisp, while the inside is beautifully tender and succulent.

Central Mexico, a land-locked area, lies to the south of Mexico City, and includes the towns of Puebla and Tlaxcala. Puebla is the home of the classic dish, *Chiles en Nogada*, which

consists of stuffed chiles dipped in batter, then fried and served with a walnut sauce. Puebla is also associated with the famous *Mole Poblano*, which was said to have been invented by nuns in a local convent. *Mole Poblano* is a wonderfully complex dish in which turkey or chicken is cooked in a paste made by mixing crushed dried chiles, cinnamon and cloves, with sesame seeds and ground nuts, as well as onion, garlic and sometimes tomatillos.

Tlaxcala, which means "the place of many tortillas," is a town renowned for its food. Chicken stuffed with fruit and nuts is one popular dish, while another consists of lamb cooked in agave leaves. Both are usually washed down with the local *pulque*.

Vast, sprawling and vibrant, Mexico City is one of the most cosmopolitan places on earth, a fact that is reflected in its food. It is often said that Mexican love to eat and would eat all day if they could, and in Mexico City there is nothing to stop them. The streets are filled with vendors selling all sorts of snacks. Some offer tortas and tortillas filled with various meats (including the chorizo for which nearby Toluca is famous), cheeses, beans and chiles. Others sell *tamales*, *sopes* and *tacos* . the commuters who rush past on their way to work. Another item available o

t other fruit for
exico City.

re served here
les and beans.

'oche, a corn
e a flavorful
been regarded
ore-Columban
cooked and used
.), which the
nto their cuisine
cupation in the

differences between
lexico, it is in the
are most marked.
o the isolation of the
r centuries cut off
e country by dense

Below: A field of corn drying on the plants.

rainforest and swampland. The Maya lived here before the conquistadors came to Mexico, and their influence on the cooking can still be seen, particularly in *pibil*-style dishes, which got their name from the *pib* or pit in which they were steamed in Mayan times.

Although the poor soil does not readily support agriculture, corn is grown in areas where the vegetation has been cut and burned, and is ground to make meal, *masa harina*, which is used for corn tortillas and a host of other Mexican dishes. The pungent herb *epazote* is used in the cooking of this region, imparting a distinctive flavor.

Good fish, squid and shellfish, including the large shrimp for which the area is well known, are available all along the coast. *Ceviche* is a popular dish, and is made from several different types of fish and shellfish, either singly or in combination.

Huevos Motuleños, a dish of eggs with refried beans and tomato sauce, is a well known Yucatec dish. Also typical of the area are dry spice pastes, called *recados*. These are mixtures of dried spices and vinegar or citrus juice, which are rubbed onto meat before it is cooked. *Recados* are made throughout the country, but they are particularly popular in the Yucatán. Some include ground achiote seed (annatto powder), which is valued for the earthy flavor and bright yellow color it imparts. Another hallmark of Yucatec cooking is the habañero, a fiery chile that is grown exclusively in the region.

MEXICAN MEAL PATTERNS

Many of the traditional Mexican dishes are very labor-intensive, reflecting the old society where the women worked all day long collecting the food required and then preparing it. Today, despite industrialization, the traditional meal patterns are still observed, especially in rural areas. Most Mexicans still eat their main meal in the middle of the day, and follow it by a siesta. Even in the cities, where meals are beginning to conform to the international pattern of breakfast, lunch and dinner, the biggest meal of the day is still eaten at lunchtime.

Desayuno

This is a light meal eaten first thing in the morning, soon after waking. It usually consists of a cup of coffee and a bread or pastry—perhaps *churros* or *pan dulce* (sweetened bread).

Almuerzo

Having started work very early in the morning, most Mexicans are ready for something fairly substantial by about 11 AM. Almuerzo is more brunch than breakfast, and usually includes an egg dish such as *Huevos Rancheros* or scrambled eggs with salsa and cheese. Tortillas are served, and coffee, milk or fruit juice washes everything down.

Comida

This is the main meal of the day, generally eaten at a leisurely pace from about 3 PM. The meal is made up of several courses. Soup is almost always served, and this is followed by a rice or pasta dish. The aptly named *platillo fuerte*—the phrase means "heavy dish"—is the main attraction. This dish is accompanied by tortillas, salad and pot beans or Refried Beans. The clay pot used to cook the pot beans—*Frijoles de Olla*—adds flavor to them. Garlic, cilantro, onion and stock with chiles are additional ingredients, and cream or cheese is stirred in just before serving. The meal closes with *postre* (dessert) and an after-dinner coffee.

Merienda

A light supper, this is often made up from the leftovers of the lunchtime *comida* dishes, which are wrapped in a tortilla to make a burrito. If a more substantial meal is required, a stew or *mole* might be served, with *Cafe con Leche* or hot chocolate to follow the food. *Merienda* is usually eaten between 8 and 9 PM.

Cena

This more elaborate meal—dinner—is served when entertaining guests in the evening or on special occasions. It replaces the *merienda* and is made up of two or three courses served any time between 8 PM and midnight.

The Main Event

Comida—the main meal of the day—provides the perfect opportunity for relaxing with family or friends. Here are some suggestions of suitable dishes to serve at this time:

Sopa

A hearty soup would not be appropriate, as this is the prelude to a large meal. *Thalpeno*, a thin soup with chicken and avocado, would be ideal, as would a cold coconut soup.

Sopa Seca

Translating as "dry soup," this is actually a rice or pasta dish, served after the conventional soup and before the main course. Rice or vermicelli is cooked in a little oil and then simmered in a broth with onions, garlic, tomatoes and other vegetables. Most of the liquid used is absorbed by the rice or pasta,

Above: Women prepare the main family meal in a rural Mexican kitchen.

Above: Prickly chayote, used in Mexican salads and vegetable dishes

Below: Green chiles for sale in a Mexican market.

hence the name. The rice dishes vary—peas are sometimes added to the basic recipe, and cilantro and chiles are used to make the popular "Green Rice." In another variation, yellow rice is flavored and colored with achiote (annatto), a golden coloring made from the ground seeds of a flowering tree.

Pescado y Legumbres

Sometimes a fish course is served before the main dish. Typically this would be Ceviche—raw fish "cooked" by the action of lime juice. Alternatively, a vegetable dish might be offered; perhaps a native vegetable such as jicama, served as a salad with a chili and lime dressing. Plantains are also popular, and either these or zucchini might be fried along with cheese and green chiles.

Platillo Fuerto

The "heavy dish" is typically a stew, served with corn tortillas and a salad. Meatballs in a tomato and chili sauce is one option; pork with green cactus sauce another. A fisherman's stew of mussels, scallops, shrimp and cod would also be suitable. For the accompaniment, a cactus or chayote salad would be ideal, or a fresh-tastin salsa of rajas con limon—strips of chil and lime.

their main meal
nt in Mexico City.

e an inevitable—
the main meal.
ed a very big part
e indigenous
r and variety of
tive. Most people,
exican bean dish,
s, which is all too
sh of badly
s. The home-
uldn't be more
is deliciously
ves, garlic and
ous are pot beans,
pinto beans put
d very slowly with
d until they are
aditionally served
lsa, sour cream and

Below: Corn on the cob is cooked and sold as a snack at street stalls.

dark brown cane sugar typical of Mexico) and stirred with a cinnamon stick. A delicious alternative, which packs more punch, is coffee with a shot of Kahlúa or tequila.

Snack Foods

Mexicans love to snack. Street food is very popular throughout the country. In towns, stalls equipped with steamers sell *tamales*—little corn husk parcels filled with spiced meat or cheese—from first thing in the morning, so that shift workers can still have their *almuerzo* even if they cannot get home. Later in the day, the stalls sell corn soup or *menudo*, a soup made with tripe. Still more stalls are set up at lunchtime by women who serve homemade food to the workforce. The food is very similar to what would be eaten at home: soup, rice or pasta dishes, stews with tortillas or bread, and desserts. In the evening, the stalls sell *quesadillas*, enchiladas and *antojitos* ("little whims"). On the coast, traders sell shrimp on skewers, *Ceviche* (marinated raw fish) threaded on sticks or *elotes*—tender ears of cooked corn dipped in cream and sprinkled generously with well-flavored crumbly cheese.

FEASTS AND FESTIVALS

Long before Christianity came to Mexico, the indigenous peoples worshipped gods whom they believed provided their food. The Aztecs were convinced that the world would come to an end unless the gods were constantly propitiated with prayers, sacrifices and rituals. Corn was regarded as a divine gift—a miraculous staple food which grew in all climates and soils.

Feast days, when people cooked particular dishes or brought specific foods as offerings to the gods, were frequent events. When Christianity spread through Mexico many of these days were appropriated by the Church and either assigned as saints' days or linked to celebrations marking important days in the religious calendar.

January 6th—*Día de los Santos Reyes*

As the culmination of two weeks of Christmas festivities, January 6th marks the meeting between the Magi—the Three Kings—and the infant Jesus. Mexicans commemorate that exchange of gifts with ceremonies of their own, and this is the day on which Christmas presents are given and received. Central to the celebration is King's Day Bread, a yeasted sweet bread ring filled with crystallized fruit, covered with icing and decorated with candied fruit jewels.

Right: Mayas in traditional dress perform a bottle dance.

Below: A Mexican dancer wearing a Spanish-influenced traditional dress.

February—Carnival

The weekend before the beginning of Lent sees the beginning of a five-day carnival, a final fling before the period of self-denial. Processions of brightly colored floats, dancing in the street and feasting are all characteristic of this celebration.

April—*Semana Santa*

Holy week—the period leading up to Easter Day—is an important time in the Mexican calendar, particularly for the many Catholics in the country. One custom peculiar to Mexico is the breaking of confetti-filled eggs over the heads of friends and family.

May 5th—*Cinco de Mayo*

This day commemorates the defeat of the French army at the Battle of Puebla in 1862. After the defeat Napoleon sent 30,000 soldiers into the country, and after a year the French had taken power. *Cinco de Mayo* is of particular importance in the state of Puebla, but is celebrated in other parts of the country and in some American states with large Mexican populations such as southern central California and Texas. Nowadays the holiday is a celebration of Mexican culture, drink and music.

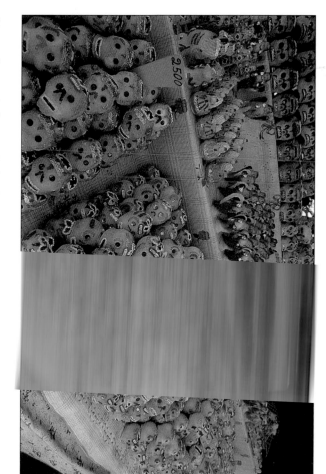

Above: Sugar skulls on sale for the celebration of one of Mexico's most important festivals, The Day of the Dead.

September 16th—Mexican Independence Day

A holiday to mark the day in 1810 when the revolt against Spanish rule began. Outside Mexico, the festival is often promoted by commercial outlets, such as Mexican restaurants and bars.

November 1 & 2—Los Días de los Muertes

Commonly called The Day of the Dead, this is in fact a two-day festival that combines in one both the ancient Aztec tradition of worship of the dead and the Christian festival of All Saints' Day.

The festival originally came about because of a widely held belief that the souls of the dead are permitted to spend a brief period on earth every year—like a vacation—to give their families a chance to spend time with them. Family members gather at the graveside, bringing the favorite foods of the deceased person, as well as other symbolic dishes that are traditionally eaten on this day. The foods include a sweet pumpkin dessert and *tamales*. At the grave candles are lit, incense is burned, special prayers are said and the food and drink are eaten in a party atmosphere. Although the festival

...it is seen by ...casion. The ...life is to be ...th is simply a

d/Christmas Day

...stmas Day, the ...rocessions— ...icting Joseph, ...y, searching for ...stmas Day sees

advertises r the festival.

the start of a two-week family holiday for most Mexicans. On the afternoon of the day itself families share a special meal. This traditionally starts with the sharing of the *rosca*—a sweet ring-shaped loaf with a small ceramic doll representing the infant Jesus baked inside it. Whoever finds the doll in their slice of cake must host a party on February 2nd, *Día de Candelaria* (Candlemas). The high point of the Christmas feast is the main course, when *Mole Poblano*, a rich turkey dish made with chiles, nuts, tomatoes, garlic, cinnamon and chocolate is served. It is accompanied by *tamales blancos*—corn husk parcels filled with a flavored mixture that is based on white cornmeal.

Mexican Weddings

These almost always take place in church. It is traditional for the bride and groom to be united during the ceremony with a *lazo*—a large rosary that is wrapped around them both. Gold or silver coins, a Bible and a rosary are given to the couple during the service by the "*padrinos*," a man and woman especially chosen by the bride and groom for this task. The coins symbolize prosperity. Mexican wedding cookies are served at the subsequent feast. Made from almonds and butter, baked and then sprinkled with confectioners' sugar, these have a shortbread-like texture.

MEXICAN COOKING OUTSIDE MEXICO

In the United States, there has been a tremendous growth in the number of Mexican restaurants and establishments serving what has come to be known as Tex-Mex food—Mexican food with a Texan influence. Sadly, these restaurants are not always very representative of the wonderful and varied cuisine Mexico has to offer, but what they have done is to stimulate interest in Mexican food and therefore a demand for more authentic Mexican ingredients and equipment. The growing popularity of Mexico among tourists has created even more of an interest in the country's varied cuisine.

United States

Mexicans who have emigrated to the United States for political, economic or personal reasons have created their own communities within that country. Parts of the United States, such as southern California and Texas, which have strong historical links to Mexico as well as sharing a common border, have large communities of Mexicans and offer some of the best Mexican food. The Mexican cuisine in these areas has evolved over time to please the palates

Below: Mexican chiles, when dried, are exported all over the world.

Above and below: Fast-food stalls serving Mexican or Tex-Mex food are a common sight all over the United States, especially in the South. These two stalls are in New Mexico.

of local residents. Authentic Mexican ingredients are used, but American products are as well. This style of cooking is often referred to as "fusion," the combining of ingredients and flavors from several cultures in one dish, a practice that carries with it the real danger of diluting each country's contribution and distorting the diners' perceptions of each cuisine. In southern California and Texas, however, authentic Mexican ingredients tend to be readily available, thanks to demand and to the proximity to the border, and improved transportation links across Mexico and into the United States ensure that products arrive fresh and undamaged.

The same cannot be said for the rest of the United States. Availability of authentic Mexican ingredients varies from state to state, and some fruits and types of chile are difficult, if not quite impossible, to obtain.

Other items, such as pinto beans, squash, avocados and chocolate, have become such an integral part of the American diet that few people would consider them to be Mexican foods.

Europe

With the growing number of European people vacationing in Mexico, the trend for new culinary flavors or experiences

and the increasing market for travel features on television and in magazines, interest in Mexican cuisine has escalated. Nowhere is this more apparent than in Scandinavia, where Mexican food is enormously popular.

Increased demand has led to more varieties of fresh and dried chiles becoming available at both major supermarkets and specialty stores, and this in turn has persuaded more people to experiment with cooking Mexican food at home. The most significant advance in recent years has been the introduction of ready-made corn and

flour tortillas at supermarkets and in heat-sealed packages that can be kept in the refrigerator until needed, when they are heated very briefly in the microwave. These have made many dishes much more accessible to the average home cook. People for whom Mexican food meant serving chile in a taco shell—and who were put off by the sheer messiness of this awkward dish—

Above: Tequila husks. Tequila has grown in popularity around the world.

Below: An American fast-food stall selling Mexican-inspired roasted corn.

Above: Chocolate is now so widespread that people don't necessarily link it with its country of origin, Mexico.

Mexican mortar and pestle) are also available by mail order, but many of the functions for which these utensils are intended are either not necessary or can be carried out just as quickly and efficiently in a food processor.

Restaurants

In America and to a lesser extent in Europe, a number of restaurant chains specializing in Mexican and Tex-Mex food have been established. Tex-Mex restaurants tend to offer burgers and steaks alongside predominantly tortilla-based dishes, so it is not surprising that many people perceive these as being all that Mexico has to offer. Even some restaurants purporting to serve authentic Mexican food perpetuate the myth that Mexicans eat plates piled high with indistinguishable mounds of food, all fairly bland, covered with melted cheese, dollops of sour cream, Guacamole and salsa. In the United States there is an increasing number of small restaurants serving authentic dishes from all over Mexico. A welcome trend indeed.

EQUIPMENT

You need very little by way of specialty equipment in order to cook Mexican food. Most modern Mexican kitchens today have a food processor to do much of the chopping and grinding. However, the items listed below will make many of the tasks easier and are worth investing in if you make a lot of Mexican food.

Tortilla Press

Traditionally, tortillas were always shaped by hand. Skilled women were able to make an astonishing number of perfectly shaped tortillas in a very short time, but this is something of a dying art today. Most people now use metal tortilla presses. Cast iron presses are the most effective, but they must be seasoned (oiled) before use and carefully cared for, so many people today prefer steel presses. These come in various sizes and are heavy, in order to limit the leverage needed to work them. Cover the plates with plastic bags or waxed paper and it will be easier to lift the tortillas once they are pressed. Tortilla presses are available at good specialty kitchenware stores and by mail order.

Comal

This is a thin, circular griddle, traditionally used over an open fire to cook tortillas. A cast iron griddle or large frying pan will do this job equally well.

Right: Tortilla press

Above: Metate

Below: Comal

Metate

A *metate* is a grinding stone used to grind corn to make *masa*. It is also used to grind cocoa and *piloncillo* (unrefined cane sugar). The design has not changed for centuries. Made from a sloping piece of volcanic rock, it has three short legs. Before a new *metate* can be used, it must be tempered. A mixture of dry rice and salt is placed on the grinding surface and the *muller*—the implement that does the actual grinding—is used to press the mixture into the surface and remove any loose pieces of sand or grit. The *muller* is made of the same stone as the *metate* and is called a *mano* or *metlapil*. These are quite difficult to locate outside Mexico, but are available by mail order.

Molcajete and Tejolote

The mortar and pestle of Mexico, the *molcajete* and *tejolote* are made from porous volcanic rock and must be tempered in the same way as the *metate* before being used. They are ideal for grinding spices such as achiote (annatto) or for grinding nuts and seeds when making *Mole Poblano*.

Tortilla Warmer

Ideal for keeping tortillas warm at the table, this is a small round basket or clay dish with a lid. The size most readily available outside Mexico is suitable for 6-inch tortillas. Look for them at specialty kitchenware stores.

Left: Dishes

Ollas

These are the clay pots traditionally used for cooking stews and sauces. They give food a unique flavor, but are seldom found outside Mexico, as they are quite fragile. Sadly, they are becoming relatively rare in Mexico too. Flat earthenware dishes decorated around the edge are used for serving and are more easily found than *ollas*.

Molinollo

A carved wooden implement used for whisking drinking chocolate. Some of these are beautiful and are popular with tourists. A wire whisk can also be used.

INGREDIENTS

Across Mexico, the very ... and variations in climate provide a remarkable range of ingredie... y resourceful, and have made good use of their native foods, as wel... the ingredients and recipes brought by successive settlers. Some c... will be familiar, others will be unusual, still more may seldom b... ntry of origin, but as the popularity of Mexican food continues... t were once rare will become increasingly commonplace. This chapt... gredients, and offers advice on purchasing, pre... well as cooking tips.

CORN

The native Indians of Mexico regarded corn as a gift from the gods. How else would they have come by such a versatile food, so hardy and adaptable and able to flourish in all the different climates and soils of their country? They offered up gifts to the god of corn, celebrated him on feast days and even added tiny grains of corn pollen to their traditional sand paintings to give the artworks healing powers. A popular myth held was that corn was in fact the very stuff from which the gods created people. Even now, corn accounts for almost 20 percent of the world's calories taken from food.

In the traditional Navajo Indian wedding ceremony, the bride's

Above: White corn

grandmother presents the couple with a basket of cornmeal and the couple exchanges a small handful with each other—such is the significance of corn in their culture.

Every part of an ear of corn is used in Mexican culture: the husks for wrapping *tamales*, the silk in medicines, the kernels for food and the stalks for animal feed. The husks from corn are most commonly used for *tamales*, but are also used for wrapping some other foods before cooking. When they are ready, the husks can be peeled off from the filling. The husks are not eaten, but are discarded once the *tamales* are cooked. In Oaxaca, *tamales* are wrapped in banana leaves, which impart a distinctively different flavor.

and adapts to different surroundings readily. There are a few main types of corn used for food, each with several different varieties.

Flint corn This is also known as Indian corn and is described as "flint" because of the hard texture of the kernel. This can be red, blue, brown or purple, which has made this type of corn a popular choice for some of the more novel foods such as blue or red corn tortilla chips. Popcorn is made from a type of flint corn. Predominantly, however, flint corn is used for industrial purposes and animal feed.

Yellow corn A type of "dent" corn, so called because the sides of the kernel are composed of a hard starch and the crown of a softer starch, which shrinks to form the characteristic depression or dent. Yellow corn has large, full-flavored kernels and is used for making many processed foods. It is also the basic ingredient used in corn syrup, cornstarch and corn oil.

White corn is used to make *masa*, a type of dough that is widely used in Mexican cooking. It may seem odd to call it white corn, when the resulting *masa* is actually quite yellow, but the kernels are noticeably whiter than those of yellow corn varieties.

Flour corn is composed largely of soft starch and can readily be ground to make flour for use in baked goods.

Varieties and Uses

Corn is the common name for a cereal grass. With wheat and rice, it is one of the world's key grain crops. A native of the Americas, it was introduced into Europe by Columbus, who brought it to Spain. A wide variety of products are produced from corn, including corn syrup, bourbon and starch.

Hybrid varieties of corn can be produced very easily, as corn mutates

Below: Red corn

Above: Blue corn

Below: Corn husks; fresh and dried

Preparing Dried Corn Husks

If you are able to buy dried corn husks you will need to make them soft and pliable before using.

Soak the corn husks in a bowl of cold water for several hours. When they are soft, remove them from the bowl and pat dry.

Place the husks flat on a dry surface. Pile on the filling, then tie in neat parcels before steaming.

Grinding produces the very white cornstarch with which we are familiar, and which is the main constituent of custard powder.

Sweet corn contains more natural sugar than other types of corn. The kernels can be eaten right off the cooked ear, and in Mexico a favorite snack is *elote con crema*, where ears of corn are dipped in cream and sprinkled with fresh cheese before being served. The kernels can also be stripped from the cobs and used in soups and vegetable dishes. As soon as the corn is picked the sugar in the kernels starts to convert to starch. This reduces the natural sweetness, so it is important

of Masa harina

Above: Wet corn being ground on the traditional metate.

In some parts of Mexico they serve blue corn *masa* dishes, using the same dough-making process, but a less common corn type.

Ingredients 25

Corn Tortillas

Have ready a tortilla press and two clean plastic bags, slit if necessary so that they will lie flat. Tortillas are more traditionally cooked on a special griddle called a *comal*, but a cast-iron griddle or large heavy frying pan will work just as well.

MAKES 12 × 6-INCH TORTILLAS

INGREDIENTS

2 cups *masa harina*

pinch of salt

1 cup warm water

1 Place the *masa harina*, salt and water in a large bowl and combine using a wooden spoon until it forms a dough.

2 Turn out the dough onto a lightly floured surface and knead well for 3–4 minutes, until firm, smooth and no longer sticky. Cover the bowl with plastic wrap and let the dough stand at room temperature for 1 hour.

3 Pinch off 12 pieces of dough of equal size and roll each piece into a ball. Work with one piece of dough at a time, keeping the rest of the pieces of dough covered with plastic wrap so that they do not dry out.

4 Open the tortilla press and place a plastic bag on the bottom. Put a dough ball on top and press with the palm of your hand to flatten slightly.

5 Lay a second plastic bag on top of the round of dough and close the press. Press down firmly several times to flatten the dough into a thin round.

6 Place a large frying pan or griddle over medium heat. Open the press and lift out the tortilla, keeping it sandwiched between the plastic bags. Carefully peel off the first bag, then gently turn the tortilla over onto the palm of your hand. Carefully peel off the second plastic bag.

7 Flip the tortilla onto the hot frying pan or griddle and cook for about 1 minute or until the lower surface is blistered and is just beginning to turn golden brown. Turn over using a spatula and keep warm until ready to serve.

8 Place a clean dish towel in a large ovenproof dish. Transfer the cooked tortilla to the dish, wrap the dish towel over the top and cover with a lid. Keep warm while you cook the remaining tortillas in the same way.

COOK'S TIP

If you do not have a tortilla press, you can improvise by placing the dough between two clean plastic bags and rolling it out with a rolling pin.

Basic *Masa*

Traditionally, tortillas are made with *masa*. *Masa* is made by mixing dried white corn with food grade calcium oxide, although this is difficult to locate in small quantities. For making tortillas, most cooks, even in Mexico, find it easier to use *masa harina*, which is the flour made when *masa* is dried and ground. *Masa harina* should not be confused with cornmeal or polenta, which are made from corn that has not been soaked or cooked with lime. The taste of tortillas made with *masa harina* is slightly different from that of tortillas made from fresh *masa*, but the flour is much easier to cook with and eliminates the need for a *metate*.

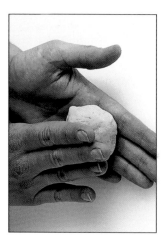

Flour Tortillas

Flour tortillas are more common than corn tortillas in the north of Mexico, especially in the areas around Sonora and Chihuahua, where wheat is grown. Flour tortillas differ from corn tortillas in that they include lard, which gives them more pliability and elasticity. For best results, make sure you use good quality all-purpose flour.

MAKES ABOUT 12 × 10-INCH TORTILLAS

INGREDIENTS

5 cups all-purpose flour, sifted

½ teaspoon baking powder

pinch of salt

scant ½ cup lard

½ cup warm water

1 Mix the flour, baking powder and salt in a large bowl. Rub in the lard, then gradually add enough water to draw the flour together into a stiff dough.

2 Turn out the dough onto a lightly floured work surface and knead it f[or] 10–15 minutes, until it is elastic.

...n a lightly floured ...gh a quarter turn ...p the round even. ...e round is about

6 Wrap the cooked tortillas in a clean, dry dish towel to keep them soft and warm while you make the rest.

12 even-size ... using the ...er the pieces ...you are working ...ng out.

eavy frying pan or ium heat. Cook one placing each one in an or on the griddle or 45 seconds–1 minute r surface begins to n. Turn over and cook or about 1 minute.

COOK'S TIPS

● If the corn tortillas crack when they are pressed, remove the dough from the press, return it to the bowl and add a little extra water.

● To reheat cold tortillas, sprinkle them with a few drops of water, wrap them in foil and place in an oven preheated to 275°F for 10 minutes. Alternatively, wrap them in plastic wrap and microwave on maximum power for about 20 seconds.

Quick and Easy Tortilla Fillings

● Cut a skinned chicken breast into thin slices and stir-fry with slices of red and yellow bell pepper. When the chicken is cooked, add the juice of a lime and some fresh oregano, add salt and pepper to taste then use the mixture to fill freshly warmed tortillas. Add some grated cheese, if desired, and a spoonful of sour cream.

● If you have some rice and refried beans left from the previous day, combine them and reheat in a frying pan with a little oil. When the mixture is thoroughly heated, spoon it into the tortillas with some grated cheese, slices of tomato and chopped scallions.

● Stir-fry some mushrooms with plenty of black pepper. Add a dash of soy sauce and a little heavy cream, season to taste, then spoon into the tortillas.

FOLDING AND COOKING TORTILLAS

Many Mexican dishes are made with tortillas. The difference lies in the filling, folding and cooking.

Burritos

These are flour tortilla envelopes enclosing various fillings and then folded into the classic shape and sealed with flour and water.

Chimichangas

A chimichanga is a burrito that has been folded, chilled to let the edges seal and then deep fried in hot oil until crisp and golden.

Chalupas

Chalupas are pieces of *masa* shaped to resemble canoes or boats and fried until opaque and golden. They are topped with beans, salsa and cheese.

Enchiladas

These can be made from either corn or wheat tortillas. A little filling is laid down the center of a tortilla, which is then rolled to make a tube, much like cannelloni. Filled tortillas are laid side by side in a baking dish before being topped with a sauce and baked or finished under the broiler.

Fajitas

These are ideal for informal dinner parties, as various fillings are placed on the table with the hot tortillas, and guests fill and roll their own. The tortilla is then folded to form a pocket around the filling.

Flautas

Corn tortillas are filled with a pork or chicken mixture, rolled tightly into flute shapes, then fried until crisp.

Quesadillas

These tasty treats are made by placing a corn or flour tortilla in a warm frying pan and spreading one half lightly with salsa. A little chicken or a few shrimp are sometimes added, and fresh cheese is sprinkled on top. The other half of the tortilla is then folded over, and the quesadilla is cooked for 1–2 minutes, during which time it is turned once.

Tacos

The crisp tortilla shells that are often sold in supermarkets as tacos are in fact a Tex-Mex invention. True Mexican tacos are corn tortillas that have been filled and folded in half; they still remain soft. *Taquitos* are miniature tacos—ideal for picnics or parties.

Tostadas

These are individual corn tortillas fried until crisp and then topped with shredded meat, Refried Beans, salsa, Guacamole, sour cream and a little fresh cheese. The finger-food versions are called *tostaditas*.

Totopos

Triangles of corn tortilla, fried until crisp, are called *totopos*. Serve them with salsa—they are delicious served while still warm.

READY-MADE TORTILLAS

Making Mexican meals is much easier than it once was, thanks to the availability of ready-made tortillas and tortilla chips.

Corn Tortillas

Many supermarkets stock 6-inch fresh corn tortillas. Look for them in the bread section. They are ideal for making tacos, tostadas, *totopos* and enchiladas. They do not have a very long shelf life, but they do freeze well. Follow the manufacturer's instructions for warming them, as methods vary.

Flour Tortillas

These are available in 6-inch, 8-inch and 10-inch rounds, and the packaging is usually marked in inches rather than centimeters. The smallest ones are perfect for fajitas or flour tortilla

Above: Corn tortillas

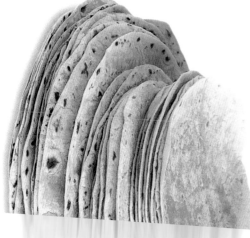

Below: Wheat flour tortillas

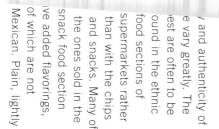

...fresh

...to be a bit
...an the fresh
...rozen. Flour
...often contain lard,
...ter than the ones
...able oil or fat.

Above: Blue and yellow tortilla chips. Plain, lightly salted chips are best for dipping with salsa.

Below: Taco shells are difficult to eat but do have their uses.

...Mex invention,
...are so awkward to
...at they are
...nsible for turning
...people off
...can food. They
...owever, an
...nt
...for
...aking
...much

...them
...nd fresh,

...y and authenticity of
...e vary greatly. The
...est are often to be
...ound in the ethnic
...food sections of
...supermarkets rather
...than with the chips
...and snacks. Many of
...the ones sold in the
...snack food section
...ve added flavorings,
...of which are not
Mexican. Plain, lightly

salted chips are best for dipping with salsa. Many specialty food stores and health food stores sell organic corn chips and naturally colored red and blue corn chips (made from colored corn kernels). These look especially good mixed with yellow corn chips in a dish. Warm them in a low oven or microwave before serving.

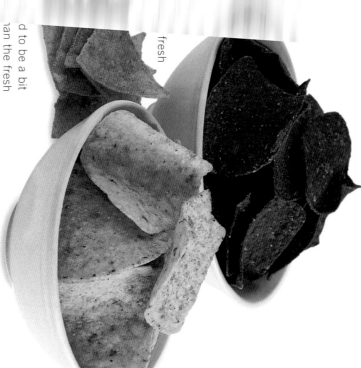

BEANS AND RICE

The importance of beans in the Mexican diet cannot really be overestimated. Indigenous to the country, they were cultivated by the Indians along with corn, and the two staple crops coexisted in a remarkable fashion. Successive plantings of corn soon deplete the soil; beans enrich it by introducing nitrogen. The early inhabitants of Mexico knew this, and planted both together. They ate them together too, and benefited from the fact that beans supplied nutrients corn lacked and, unlike corn, were also an excellent source of protein. Rice was first introduced to Mexico by the Spanish and is also an important staple ingredient.

BEANS

Beans continue to be a staple food in Mexico, and there is a pot of dried beans simmering daily on the stove in many homes. Fresh beans are eaten, too, of course, but it is the dried beans, with their better keeping properties, that are most widely used. They make a colorful display on market stalls, and there are many different varieties to choose from.

Popular Varieties

Pinto beans and black beans are the most commonly used dried beans in Mexico, although lima beans, which are sold both fresh and dried, are used in a number of dishes and side dishes.

Chickpeas, which in Mexico are called garbanzos, are not native to the country but were brought in from the Middle East. They have become popular, however, and feature in several dishes.

Pinto beans Pinto is Spanish for "painted" and refers to the speckles of red-brown on the pale pink skins. These beans are native to Latin America and are now widely used in most Spanish-speaking countries. A rich source of protein and iron, they are only available dried. Mexicans use them for all sorts of dishes, but it is as *Frijoles de Olla*, the simple bean dish that is eaten daily in most homes, that they are most familiar. The cooked beans are also the basis of *Refritos* (Refried Beans), and are used in salsas.

Black beans Small, with black skin and cream-colored flesh, these beans have a wonderfully sweet flavor. Do not confuse them with black-eyed peas, which are white, with a small black eye. The glossy skins look particularly attractive after cooking. They are used in soups and salsas, and are often substituted for pinto beans in *Frijoles de Olla*. Despite their small size, black beans can take quite a long time to

Above: Pinto beans

soften when cooked, so always test before draining to ensure that they are perfectly tender.

Buying and Storing

Dried beans keep very well, but not indefinitely, so it is best to buy them in relatively small quantities, at a store with rapid turnover. That way, they are likely to be tender and full of flavor when soaked and cooked, unlike beans that have been kept for too long, which become dry and so hard that they are only fit for use as weights in pie crusts. Store beans in tightly closed containers in a cool, dry place.

Preparation

Before you use dried beans, put them in a colander or sieve and pick them over, removing any foreign bodies, then rinse them thoroughly under cold running water. Drain, transfer to a large bowl and pour in plenty of cold water.

Above: Black beans.

Let soak for several hours and preferably overnight. Alternatively, you can boil the beans in plenty of water for 3–4 minutes, then cover the pan and set it aside for an hour before cooking. This is very useful when you have forgotten to soak beans for a particular dish, although the long cold soak is preferable.

Main Uses and Cooking Tips

In Mexico, beans are widely used in soups, as fillings for tortillas, in many meat dishes and on their own, either freshly cooked or refried.

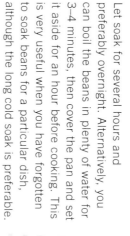

To cook pre-soaked dried beans, simply drain them thoroughly, then put them in a clean pan with plenty of water. Do not add salt, as this would cause the skins on the beans to toughen. Bring the water to a boil and then cook for the time recommended in the individual recipes, usually 1–1¼ hours.

Right: Long-grain (top) and ground r[ice]...

onsiderably, so
ss before
ng the beans.

ng rice since it
ountry by the
tury. It was
xico from the
o shipped on

ed in

that each grain is four times longer than its width. White long-grain rice that has had the husk removed is most common, although it is often not as refined as the white rice most widely sold in the West.

Buying and Storing

Most rice for sale in the West comes in packages. It keeps extremely well in a cool, dry place, but once packages are opened, any unused rice should be transferred to an airtight container and used as soon as possible. For Mexican food, it is important to use rice that absorbs the flavors of other ingredients well. It is customary to use ordinary long-grain rice, but you may want to experiment with other types.

Main Uses and Cooking Tips

Rice is used in a variety of Mexican dishes, from *sopa seca* (dry soup), which is served as a separate course in the *comida* or main meal, to rice pudding. When served as an accompaniment, rice is usually mixed with other ingredients, as in the popular Green Rice, which includes chiles, and Yellow Rice, which owes its color to achiote (annatto). Ground rice is used as a flour (*harina de arroz*) in cakes and cookies. *Horchata* is a drink made with rice that has been soaked and then finely ground. Most Mexicans tend to soak their rice in boiled water for a minimum of 10 minutes before they cook it. This reduces the cooking time and also encourages the rice to absorb other flavors. After soaking, it should be drained thoroughly before being cooked.

CHOCOLATE, NUTS AND SEEDS

Candy, cookies, cakes and pastries are much loved by the Mexicans, but the sweet ingredients that go into these are also used in savory dishes, and chocolate, along with various types of nuts and seeds, is a very important element of Mexican cooking.

CHOCOLATE

When the Spanish reached Mexico, they discovered a wealth of unfamiliar ingredients, including potatoes, vanilla, avocados and squash. One of their greatest finds, however, was chocolate. The Aztecs were very partial to a drink made from the beans of the cacao tree, which they flavored in many different ways, and the Spanish, like the rest of the world after them, embraced this wonderful new taste with enthusiasm,

developing a fondness for a variation that included corn, honey and spices.

The conquistadors took chocolate back to Spain, and it was not long before all the most fashionable resorts and cities in Europe boasted cocoa houses. Initially it was served as a drink, but Spanish women also prepared it as candy, mixing it with sugar, cinnamon, eggs and almonds. Europeans started producing chocolate in slabs some two hundred years later, but women in Guatemala began pressing chocolate powder into bars for storage some time before this. When slabs of chocolate were finally produced in Mexico, the chocolate was sweetened and spiced in Spanish style.

Mexican Chocolate

This is made using dark and bitter chocolate mixed with sugar, ground nuts and cinnamon, and pressed into disks. The chocolate has a grainy quality, thanks to the sugar and almonds, and is crumbly when broken. One of the most popular brands is *Ibarra*, which comes in a distinctive yellow hexagonal box. Some specialty suppliers outside Mexico stock this product.

Buying and Storing

Mexican chocolate comes in packages, each containing five or six disks that are wrapped individually in waxed paper. Check the package for a use-by date. Store in a cool, dry place.

Making Mexican Chocolate

If you cannot buy Mexican chocolate, you can still make an acceptable substitute, using dark bitter chocolate with a minimum of 70 percent cocoa solids.

Break 4 ounces dark chocolate into pieces and put it in a food processor. Add ¼ cup ground almonds, ¼ cup sugar and 2 teaspoons ground cinnamon. Process into a fine powder, then transfer into an airtight container, close the lid tightly and store in the refrigerator for up to 2 weeks, using as needed.

Main Uses and Cooking Tips

The main use for chocolate in Mexico is still as a beverage. Mexicans are very partial to *Champurrada*, a chocolate corn drink, and the classic Mexican Hot Chocolate, which is whisked into a froth with a special whisk called a *molinollo*. Mexican Hot Chocolate is served with *Churros*, long fritters that are dunked in the drink, or *Pan Dulce*, the sweet bread that Mexicans eat for breakfast or as a snack late in the day. The extra ingredients make Mexican chocolate unsuitable for *moles*, the rich stews to which chocolate is traditionally added, so bitter chocolate or cocoa is used.

Left: Ibarra chocolate

NUTS AND SEEDS

The three types of nut that are most widely used in Mexican cooking are the pecan, walnut and almond. Pine nuts are used in some desserts and pastries, and coconuts are valued both for their flesh and the cooling liquid they contain. Pecans grow in Northern Mexico. Walnuts, which were introduced from Europe, are cultivated in the colder, central highlands. The Spanish introduced almonds into Mexican cooking during the colonial era, but ensured that the trade with Spain was not disrupted by making it illegal for Mexicans themselves to cultivate them on a large scale.

Seeds from various types of pumpkin and squash have been important ingredients in Mexican cooking for centuries. At one time, pumpkins were grown mainly for their seeds; the flesh was discarded. Sesame seeds are also used, both in pastes and as a garnish on dishes such as *Mole Poblano*.

Buying and Storing

All types of nuts have a limited shelf life once they have been shelled. The oil in them quickly turns rancid, so they

...sl...
...s...
...fr...
...p...
...h...

...e

...eeded, and

whole,
in sweet and
soups.
...nds to thicken
ground almonds
and cookies.
...n cookies,
Nuez, which are
...ristmas time
...Walnuts). They
...ishes such as
...ut Sauce (*Chiles
...alted pumpkin
...served as snacks,
...d pumpkin seeds
...in sauces such as
Pumpkin Seed
Pine nuts, known
...n seeds in Mexico,
...ed to dishes like
...and are also
...r use in desserts

*...wise from top left:
...eds, sesame seeds*

Roasting Seeds

When dry-roasting or toasting pumpkin or sesame seeds, watch them carefully so that they do not burn. Use a heavy pan placed over low heat, and stir or shake the pan frequently to keep the seeds on the move at all times. If they are allowed to burn, they will taste bitter and will spoil the flavor of any dish to which they are added.

Above: Pecans, almonds and walnuts

PILONCILLO—MEXICAN SUGAR

Mexico produces an unrefined brown cane sugar called *piloncillo*. It comes in small cones and adds a distinctive flavor and color to any dish to which it is added. Unfortunately, *piloncillo* is still not readily available outside Mexico, but brown sugar can be used in recipes as a substitute.

FRUITS

Visit any Mexican market and what will strike you first are the colorful displays of fruit of every size, shape and color. Some, such as mangoes, papayas and limes, will be familiar, but others may not look or taste like anything you have ever seen before. Fruit is an important part of the Mexican diet, providing the vitamins to balance the corn and beans that are the staple foods. Most of the fruit consumed in Mexico is grown in the country, and some of the surplus is exported to Europe.

CITRUS FRUIT

All types of citrus grow well in Mexico, and because the fruit is allowed to ripen naturally on the trees, it tends to have a very good flavor.

Description and Varieties

Limes have very thin skins, which would eventually turn yellow if they were left on the tree long enough. The pulp is green and juicy. Mexican limes—limones—are smaller than other varieties. Almost round in shape, they taste very aromatic. **Lemons** are more oval, and have thicker skins with a dense layer of white pith just below the surface. Their pulp is yellow and acidic, but tastes markedly different than that of lime.

Oranges grow well in Mexico and freshly squeezed orange juice is widely available, especially in the south. The fruits tend to look much paler than their brightly colored counterparts in American markets, but are very sweet and juicy.

Buying and Storing

Mexican limes are seldom available outside the country, but any other type of lime can be substituted in recipes. Select limes with smooth, dark green skins, and avoid any that look wizened. The fruit should be heavy for its size. Small brown patches on the skin are harmless and will not affect the flavor or the juiciness of the fruit. Store uncut limes in a plastic bag in the refrigerator or a cool room. They will keep for up to 10 days in their peak condition.

Lemons should be plump, with unblemished bright yellow skins. Avoid any whose skins are tinged with green, as this would indicate that the fruit is under-ripe.

Oranges should feel heavy for their size. Avoid any that are damaged, shriveled or have moldy skins. Oranges keep well at room temperature.

Below: Lemons and limes

Above: Oranges

Preparation

The zest on citrus fruit is often thinly pared or grated and used for decoration or flavoring. When paring the zest, take care to remove only the colored outer layer, leaving the bitter white pith behind. The pith must be removed before the fruit is sliced or segmented.

Main Uses and Cooking Tips

Limes, lemons and oranges are used extensively in cooking. Both lime and lemon juice are used to preserve vegetables, as in Onion Relish (*Cebollas en Escabeche*) and are added to casseroles, fruit platters and fresh vegetable dishes to heighten the natural flavors. The most famous use of limes—other than with tequila—is in *Ceviche*. Raw fish or shellfish is marinated in the juice until the texture of the flesh changes, becoming as firm and white as if it had been cooked. Citrus juices are also used to prevent vegetables or fruits, such as avocados, from discoloring on contact with the air. The skins of oranges, lemons or limes are often ground, and the oil is used as a flavoring.

GRANADILLAS

These fruits are the largest members of the passion fruit family. Native to South America, they are round, with a small stem attached at one end, so that they resemble Christmas tree ornaments. The tough, shell-like outer skin is bright orange, while the pulp inside is green and very seedy. It smells and tastes like citrus fruit and is not as fragrant as the pulp of the smaller, purplish-black passion fruit.

Buying and Storing

Unlike passion fruit, which are wrinkled and dimpled when ripe, granadillas should be smooth, with no marks. They can be stored at room temperature for up to 1 week. When ripe, the pulp is moist and juicy, but it dries out if they are stored for too long.

Preparation

Cut the fruit in half and scoop out the pulp with a teaspoon. The seeds are edible, but sieve the pulp if you prefer.

Main Uses and Cooking Tips

Granadilla pulp can be used in desserts, either with the seeds, or sieved. It is often poured over ice cream or fruit salad, either on its own or in a dessert sauce. It also makes a superb fruit drink, and the sieved pulp is often mixed with fresh orange juice.

Right: Granadillas

G[UAVAS] / [Guayabas]

[...] ll eaten [...] served alone or as [...] resh, soft cheeses.

[...]rably in color, [...] variety most [...] the yellow guava. [...] yellow guava has a [...]t particularly [...]nt smell. The skin is [...]hick, and is referred [...]e shell. Inside is a [...] pulp, which is full of [...] seeds. The flesh has [...]clean, sweet, slightly [...] acidic flavor.

Preparation

Cut the fruit in half and scrape out the flesh with a spoon. The seeds can be eaten, or the pulp can be pressed through a sieve, if preferred.

Buying and Storing

Guavas should be bought when they are still firm and unblemished. You will find that under-ripe fruit will ripen quite quickly at room temperature. Ripe [...]ever, should be kept in [...]ce—or in the [...]oom temperature. Ripe [...] guavas readily ferment [...]ecome inedible.

Main Uses and Cooking Tips

Guavas are usually used in desserts, but their flavor is such that they are equally good in savory dishes. Sweet guava sauces are served with cakes; savory ones are excellent with fish.

In Mexico, guava flesh is often boiled with sugar, lemon juice, cinnamon and other spices to make a thick fruit purée. The purée is then poured into a shallow dish and left to cool, then cut into pieces to eat either on its own or with cheese. The fruit is also made into a preserve or relish.

Left: Guavas

MANGOES

Perhaps the most popular of all tropical fruits, mangoes have a wonderful perfume when ripe. The buttery flesh can be absolutely delicious, although some Mexican mangoes have a slightly resinous flavor.

Description and Varieties

There are thousands of varieties of mango. All start off green, but most will change to yellow, golden or red when they are ripe.

Buying and Storing

The best way of telling whether a mango is ripe is to sniff it. It should have a highly perfumed aroma. Next, press it lightly. If it is ripe, the fruit will just yield under your fingertips. Mangoes will ripen at home if placed in a paper bag with a banana. Eat them as soon as they are ripe.

Preparation

It has been said that the best way to eat a mango is in the bath. Failing that, use a sharp knife to take a lengthwise slice off either side of the fruit, as close to

the pit as possible. Scoop out the flesh from each slice, then cut the rest of the flesh off the pit so that none is wasted.

Main Uses and Cooking Tips

Mexicans eat mangoes just as they are, but also use them in a range of desserts and drinks, with or without alcohol. A wonderful way to enjoy mango is in a Mango and Peach Margarita.

PINEAPPLES

Pineapples originated in South America and were introduced to other tropical areas by the Spanish and Portuguese. Historians have found records that prove that pineapples were cultivated by the indigenous peoples of Mexico long before the Spanish conquest.

Description and Varieties

Pineapples have hard, scaly skin and a crown of green leaves on top. The color of the skin varies. Although most ripe pineapples are yellow or orange, some, such as the Sugar Loaf that grows in Mexico, are green when fully ripe. The flesh is yellow and very juicy, with a sweet flavor that can be tangy or even slightly tart.

Above: Mangoes

Preparing a Mango

1 Place the mango narrow side down on a cutting board. Cut off a thick lengthwise slice, keeping the knife as close to the pit as possible. Turn the mango around and repeat on the other side. Cut off the flesh adhering to the pit.

2 Score the flesh on each thick slice with criss-cross lines at ½-inch intervals, taking care not to cut through the skin.

3 Fold the mango halves inside out. The flesh will stand proud, in neat cubes. Slice these off, or, for a "hedgehog," leave attached and serve.

Pineapple

that is slightly
strong color
ves.
picked ripe, as
nvert to sugar
cked.
rator for up to

eliciously
ved quite
ple is often
d in desserts
ory dishes as
Pineapple juice
, and is widely
the fresh fruit
d sold by

Preparing a Pineapple

1 Use a sharp knife to cut off the green leaves that form the crown and discard it.

2 With a sharp knife, remove the skin from the pineapple cutting deeply enough to remove most of the "eyes."

3 Use a small knife to take out carefully any "eyes" that remain in the pineapple flesh.

4 Cut the pineapple lengthwise into quarters and remove the core section from the center of each piece. Chop the pineapple flesh or cut it into slices and use as needed.

PRICKLY PEARS

Prickly pears are the fruits of several different types of cactus. Popular all over South America, they grow wild and are also cultivated, and serve as a staple food in some of the poorer rural areas of Mexico. The fleshy leaves of prickly pears—nopales—are treated as a vegetable, and you will find more information about them under the heading of Fruit Vegetables in the latter part of this introduction.

Description

Prickly pears are shaped like grenades and range in color from deep red to greenish orange. Their name is well earned, for the tough outer skin has tiny tufts of hairs or prickles, which can be very sharp. The fruit is valued for its pulp, which has a sweet aromatic flavor, much like that of melons, but even more subtle. The pulp contains small brown seeds, which are edible raw, but which become hard when cooked.

Right: Prickly pears

Buying and Storing

To tell whether a prickly pear is ripe, squeeze it carefully (avoiding the prickles!). Do not buy soft fruit or under-ripe fruit, which is dark green in color and very hard. Fruit that is slightly firm will ripen if left at room temperature for a few days.

Preparation

The prickles on these fruit are usually removed before they are sold, but if not, they can be scrubbed off with a stiff brush before the fruit is peeled. It is essential to wear kitchen gloves while carrying out this operation.

Main Uses and Cooking Tips

The peeled fruit should be halved and the flesh scooped out with a teaspoon. It can be strained and used as a sauce, or the fruit can be served as part of a fruit platter. Lime juice and chili powder are sometimes added to enliven the flavor. Prickly pears can also be made into jelly or jam.

Peeling Prickly Pears

1 Having scrubbed off the prickles, put on a pair of kitchen gloves and hold the fruit down with one hand while you cut off the skin.

2 Alternatively, hold down the prickly pear with a fork and cut a thin slice from the top and bottom of the fruit, then slit the fruit from top to bottom on either side. Peel off the skin, then cut the flesh and arrange on a plate, or simply eat the pear whole.

3 If you prefer, cut the pear in half without removing the skin and scoop out the flesh with a teaspoon. You can eat the flesh in this way as you scoop, or transfer the pulp to a bowl and serve with lime juice.

Above: Coconut

Other Tropical Fruit Treats

Other fruits popular in Mexico include **papayas**, which are valued for the tenderizing qualities of their skins, as well as that delicious flesh. These pear-shaped fruits, with vivid yellow skins, are also used in drinks sold by street vendors to quench commuters' thirsts on hot afternoons. Mexicans eat fruit with ground chiles and lime juice as a snack, or part of a meal and slices of papaya are often included. The peppery, round black seeds are edible but are seldom used in dishes. **Pomegranates**, which are used in sauces including the famous dish of Stuffed Chiles in a Walnut

Above: Papayas

Nagada, which ... ...ecial occasions. ...used in refreshing ...cas sold by street ...y to use the seeds ...ng white pith. ...s honey-colored ...illa-flavored **nuts** are grown in ...eces are often sold ...th ice water on ...towns. A chilled ...made in the ...s. One of the most ...ico is the **sapote**, ...on-pink flesh. It is ...r cloying, but ...rmalade, which ...s for its alternative ...e of marmalade ...m.

Preparing a Pomegranate

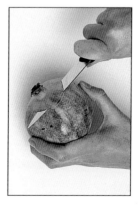

1 Cut off a thin slice from one end.

2 Stand the fruit upright. Cut downward through the skin at intervals, using a small sharp knife.

3 Bend back the segments and use your fingers to push the seeds into a bowl.

4 Remove all the bitter pith and membrane and use as needed.

FRUIT VEGETABLES

There are some fruits that are used so often in savory dishes that we tend to think of them as vegetables. Tomatoes are the obvious example, but avocados, bell peppers and chiles also are in this category. Mexico seems to have more than its fair share of these fruit vegetables, including the tomatillo, which is often called the Mexican green tomato, although it is actually related to the cape gooseberry.

AVOCADOS

It is believed that the Aztecs introduced avocado seedlings to Mexico during the 13th and 14th centuries, calling them *ahuacatl*, a name whose Spanish version was first corrupted to alligator pear and then to the name by which the fruit vegetable is known today.

Description and Varieties

There are several varieties of avocado. Most are pear-shaped and contain a central pit. The flesh ranges in color from creamy yellow to bright green and has a buttery texture and mild but distinctive flavor.

Avocado Leaves

In Mexico and other countries where the fruit flourishes, fresh or dried avocado leaves are used for their flavoring properties, much as bay leaves are used elsewhere. They can either be crushed and added to

Left: Avocado

knobbly black skins that are almost shell-like. Hass avocados have creamy flesh and a very good flavor. Another variety is the fuerte avocado, which has glossy green skin and yellow-green flesh.

The indigenous Mexican avocado has fragrant green flesh around a large pit. The thin skin can be eaten, which is unusual, since most avocados have skins that are tough and inedible, and some, like the Hass variety, have

dishes or put in whole and then removed just before the dish is served. Dried avocado leaves are usually toasted before being added to dishes such as Refried Beans, stews and marinades or used for meat that is going to be broiled or grilled.

Buying and Storing

To confirm that an avocado is ripe, press the top end of the fruit gently. It should just yield. If it is soft, the fruit is over-ripe, will prove messy to peel and will have flesh that is soft and mushy. Avocados that are bruised will have blackened flesh.

Finding the perfect avocado is partly a matter of luck, however. Even if you have chosen carefully and have taken great care not to let the fruit get bruised on the journey from the store to your home, the flesh may still be flecked with brownish spots when you finally cut it open.

Store ripe avocados in the refrigerator; under-ripe fruit will ripen if left for a few days in a warm room. Cut avocados discolor quickly. Although this process can be delayed slightly, it is advisable not to prepare the fruit until you are ready to serve it.

Main Uses and Cooking Tips

Avocados are used extensively in Mexican cookingy, most famously in Guacamole, the mashed avocado dip. They are also used in soups—both hot and cold—or to make a hot sauce for meat. Fresh avocado tastes wonderful in salads and with seafood. It is often used in tortilla dishes and is also a favorite ingredient in a range of *tortas*—Mexican sandwiches.

As soon as an avocado is cut, the flesh begins to blacken. Sprinkling the slices or chunks with lemon or lime juice delays the process somewhat, and Mexicans swear that burying the avocado pit in the mashed avocado flesh has the same effect.

Guacamole

Guacamole originated in Mexico, but has become one of the world's most popular dishes. Mashed avocado is the main ingredient, but other items, such as onion, garlic, diced tomato, chopped chiles, lime or lemon juice as well as seasonings are added. The smooth, buttery taste of the avocado gives this dip a creamy texture, yet it contains no saturated fat. Guacamole is often served with tortilla chips as a simple dip. It is an essential accompaniment to fajitas, is used in *tortas*, and is served alongside meat and fish dishes.

Simple Guacamole

1 Cut two avocados in half. Remove the pits and scoop the flesh out of the shells. Place it in a blender and process until almost smooth. Transfer into a bowl and add the juice of half a lime.

2 Add one-quarter of a small onion, chopped finely, a crushed garlic clove and a handful of cilantro, also chopped finely.

3 Add salt and other seasoning to taste and serve immediately, with tortilla chips for dipping. The Guacamole will keep in the refrigerator for 2–3 days if it is kept in an airtight container.

VARIATION

Try adding chopped fresh tomatoes and fresh chile to give your Guacamole added flavor, texture and fire.

1 For avocado slices, cut the fruit in half, remove the pit, then nick the skin at the top of each half and ease it away until you can peel off the skin completely; if the avocado is ripe, it will come off cleanly and easily.

avocado halves
n a small, sharp
nd the fruit,
l cutting right in
s the pit.

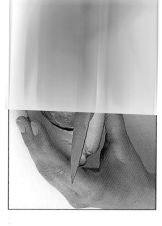

o halves apart

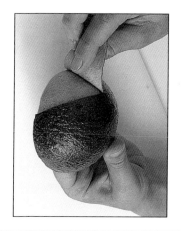

2 Cut the peeled avocado halves into slices, leaving them attached at one end if you want to fan them on the plate. Sprinkle them with lemon or lime juice to stop them from discoloring too quickly.

ade into the pit,
any of the brown
:mains on the
ove it. The
n be served with
ith shrimp or
ices of ham.
esh can be
vl and mashed.

1 For cubes of avocado, score the half of avocado and then with the tip of the knife gently lift each cube out one by one.

Left: Tomatoes

TOMATOES

Tomatoes are native to western South America and were cultivated by the Aztecs long before the Spanish invasion. Hernando Cortés is credited with introducing the first tomatoes—yellow ones—to Europe. They were initially treated with suspicion, but after a pair of Jesuit priests introduced red tomatoes to Italy in the 18th century, they steadily become more and more popular.

Description and Varieties

There are numerous varieties of tomato, ranging from tiny cherry tomatoes to ridged beefsteak tomatoes that measure as much as 4 inches across. Great piles of plum tomatoes are a common sight at Mexican markets. Richly flavored, with fewer seeds than most other varieties, they are a popular choice for salads and salsas.

Buying and Storing

Tomatoes sold in Mexican markets will have ripened naturally, and will be full of flavor, so use ripe home-grown tomatoes or vine tomatoes when cooking Mexican dishes. Over-ripe tomatoes can be used for soups or purées, but avoid any tomatoes that show signs of mold. Avoid buying tomatoes that are still green, but pale ones that have begun to redden can be ripened in a brown paper bag, especially if you add a slice of apple. Try to either store fresh tomatoes at room temperature, or bring them to room temperature before use, as chilling dulls the flavor.

Preparation

If a recipe requires that a tomato be seeded, just cut it in half and squeeze gently, or scoop out the seeds with a teaspoon. To peel, cut a cross in the bottom of the tomato, immerse it in boiling water for 3 minutes, then plunge into cold water. Drain well. The skins will have begun to peel back from the crosses and will be easy to remove. Chop or slice the tomatoes, as needed for individual recipes. If sliced tomatoes are called for, it is better to slice them across, rather than downward.

Main Uses and Cooking Tips

Mexicans use tomatoes in so many of their recipes that it would be impossible to list them all. They feature in both hot and cold soups, salsas, salads and meat and fish dishes. Chopped tomatoes are added to beans to make *frijoles*, are mixed with avocados in Guacamole and are used in Sangrita, a popular drink that is sipped alternately with tequila.

TOMATILLOS/TOMATE VERDE

Despite the name by which we know them—and the fact that they are sometimes referred to as Mexican green tomatoes—tomatillos are not members of the tomato family. Instead, they are related to cape gooseberries, those pretty little orange fruit surrounded by papery lanterns, which are so popular for garnishing. They have been grown in Mexico since Aztec times, when they were known as *miltomatl*. Mexicans seldom use the term "tomatillo," preferring to call these fruit by one of their many local names, which include *fresadilla* and *tomate milpero*.

Description

Ranging in color from yellowish green to lime, tomatillos are firm, round fruit, about the size of a small tomato, but lighter in weight, as they are not juicy. Fresh ones usually have the brown

---

Quick Fresh Tomato Salsa

A quick and easy tomato salsa, which can be prepared in minutes. Serve as a side dish with meat or fish, or as a simple appetizer with a pile of tortilla chips.

INGREDIENTS

3 fresh tomatoes, chopped
1 red onion, finely chopped
1 clove of garlic, crushed
½ green bell pepper, finely chopped
1 tablespoon chopped jalapeño or fresno chile, finely chopped
2 tablespoons chopped cilantro
3 tablespoons fresh lime juice
salt and ground black pepper to taste

1 Place the tomatoes, onion, garlic, green pepper and chile in a large bowl and combine.

2 Add the chopped cilantro and fresh lime juice, then taste and season with salt and ground black pepper to taste. Serve immediately or transfer to an airtight container and store in the refrigerator.

Fresh tomatillos with husks

papery husk attached to them at the stem end. The flavor ... resembles that of tart apples with a hint of lemon, and is enhanced by cooking, although a *salsa cruda* of raw tomatillos has a very pleasant, clean taste.

Buying and Storing

Fresh tomatillos are difficult to come by outside Mexico, but some specialty stores sell them, and they are also available by mail order in season. They can also be grown from seed, a most worthwhile enterprise for anyone who loves their clean, slightly acidic flavor. If you do locate a supply of fresh tomatillos, look for firm fruit with tight-fitting husks, and store them in the refrigerator for up to 1 week.

In the same way that canned carrots bear little resemblance to fresh ones, canned tomatillos are softer and not as tasty as fresh, but they are more

Above: Canned tomatillos

Salsa Cruda de Tomatillo

1 To make a rough textured salsa with tomatillos, process 1 pound fresh tomatillos in a food processor or chop them finely, then mix with one chopped small onion and one crushed garlic clove. Add two seeded and chopped jalapeño chiles and salt to taste.

2 Finely chop a small bunch of cilantro and add it to the tomatillo mixture.

3 Stir well, spoon into a clean bowl and serve immediately with freshly made corn tortilla chips.

Ingredients 43

Right: Plantains

PLANTAINS

Native to Southeast Asia, plantains are popular in many Latin American countries, and particularly those that have a coastline on the Caribbean.

Description and Varieties

Plantains are a type of banana, larger than the sweet bananas and with a harder skin. There are several varieties, all initially green, but some ripening to yellow, then black, while others become dark pink or red when ripe. The flesh is fibrous and starchy and must be cooked before being eaten. The flavor can be quite mild, resembling that of a squash, but when plantains are fried, the flesh tastes sweeter and has a more obvious banana flavor.

Buying and Storing

Both green and ripe plantains are used in cooking. Look for them at markets specializing in West Indian or African foods. Ripe plantains are slightly soft to the touch. If a recipe calls for ripe plantains, and you can only get green or yellow ones, they will ripen if left in a warm room for a couple of days. Unlike sweet bananas, ripe plantains can be stored in the refrigerator for a day or two.

Preparation

Plantains can't simply be peeled, like bananas. Removing the flesh can be quite tricky, unless they are very ripe. The best way to do it is to cut the plantains into short lengths, then slit the skin along one of the natural ridges so that it can be eased apart and removed. Unless you are going to use the peeled plantains immediately, put them in a bowl of acidulated water (water to which lime juice has been added) to prevent them from discoloring. When slicing plantains for chips, don't remove the skins first. Put the slices into a bowl of salted water for about half an hour, then drain them. It will be quite easy to press the slices of plantain out of their skins.

Main Uses and Cooking Tips

Plantains are used in both sweet and savory dishes. Fried plantain slices are delicious with a chili dip or simply a squeeze of lime and a sprinkling of chili powder. Slices can be cooked in butter and served as a vegetable, the sweet creaminess making them a good partner for a hot, spicy dish. They are good in meat dishes, but make a delectable dessert. Just cook them in butter and cinnamon, with a little sugar and a good amount of rum.

Banana Leaves

In parts of Mexico, banana leaves are used instead of corn husks for wrapping food before cooking. Before use, the leaves should be soaked in water until soft, then dried on paper towels. They will impart a unique, slightly lemony flavor to food cooked in them.

SWEET BELL PEPPERS

Sometimes known as capsicums, these are native to Mexico and Central America, and were also a staple food for the Incas in Peru.

Description

Sweet peppers range in color from green through yellow and orange to deep red, depending on ripeness, and there is even a purplish-black variety. They have a mild, sweet flavor and crisp, juicy flesh. Peppers can be eaten raw or cooked.

Buying and Storing

When buying peppers, try to look for specimens with bright, glossy skins. Avoid any that are limp or wrinkled, or that have "blistered" areas on the skin. Store them in a cool place or in the refrigerator for up to 1 week.

Preparation

Inside each pepper is a core that is surrounded by seeds, which must be removed. If the peppers are to be used whole, this can be lifted out if a neat slice is taken off the top, around the stem. If the peppers are halved or quartered, removing the core and seeds is even easier. Many Mexican recipes call for peppers to be roasted over a gas

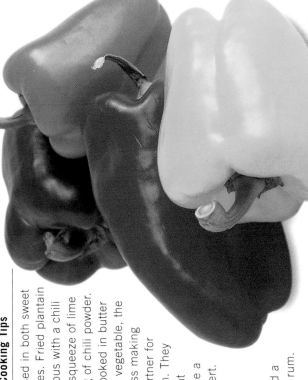

Right: Sweet bell peppers

Preparing Peppers

1 For peppers to be served whole, use a sharp knife to cut a ring around the stem at the top of each pepper. Lift out the core and surrounding seeds. If the peppers can be cut into halves or quarters, do this taking care not to cut into the core, then cut around it and remove.

2 For roasted peppers, roast over a gas flame or in a dry frying pan or griddle.

3 Place them in a strong plastic bag and seal the bag. Leave until the steam loosens the skin. Remove the skin and slice or chop the peppers.

Preparing *Nopales*

1 Wearing gloves or holding each paddle in turn with kitchen tongs, cut off the bumps that contain the thorns with a sharp knife. Try not to remove the whole of the green outer surface; just the parts containing spines.

2 Cut off and discard the thick base of each paddle. Rinse the paddles well and either chop them or cut them into strips.

Main Uses

Nopales are used in stews and soups, particularly in the Tlaxcala area of Mexico, and are pickled for use in salsas and salad dishes. They are even added to scrambled eggs.

Cooking Nopales

Cactus can be slimy when cooked. Mexican cooks often add onion and garlic at the start of cooking, removing them after the sliminess has gone. You can also boil *nopales* in water, drain them, then rinse under cold water. Cover with a damp dish towel and leave for 30 minutes, by which time the gumminess will have disappeared.

CHILES

Chiles have been grown in South America for thousands of years. Over 150 indigenous varieties are found in Mexico alone. In 1942 Columbus brought chiles to Europe, and from there they spread around the world.

Mexican food is often perceived as being very hot, and some of the dishes certainly live up to their reputation, but it is possible to find many dishes that are only mildly flavored with chiles. The heat level of a chile is determined by the amount of capsaicin it contains. This compound is concentrated mainly in the ribs and seeds, so you can reduce the fieriness considerably by removing these parts. Chiles that have been pickled, or that are used raw, tend to have more heat than cooked chiles.

The heat level of a chile is measured in Scoville units, on a scale where 0 is the heat level of a sweet pepper and 300,000 is the hottest chile, the habañero. In many instances, the ratings have been simplified to a scale of 1–10, to make them easier to remember.

The heat level of a particular chile will vary according to where it was grown, when it was picked, the weather during the growing season and a host of other factors, so Scoville units can only be a guide. Each crop from the same plant will be different.

Fresh Chiles

The following are the most commonly used fresh chiles:

Serrano Heat level 8. This is a small chile, about 1½–2 inches long and ½ inch wide, with a pointed tip. Serrano chiles change from green to red when ripe, and are sold at both stages of their development. The flavor is clean and biting. Serranos are used in cooked dishes, Guacamole and salsas.

Jalapeño Heat level 6. One of the most common—and most popular—types of chile, this is about the same length as a serrano, but plumper. Jalapeños are sold at all stages of ripeness, so you are as likely to find red as green. Green jalapeños are often pickled. One method of preparing jalapeños is to stuff with fresh cheese, coat in a light batter and deep-fry.

Poblano Heat level 3. Like many chiles, poblanos are initially green, and ripen to a dark red. They are large chiles, being roughly 3½ inches long

Left: Poblana chiles

Below: Jalapeño and serrano chiles

Roasting and Peeling Chiles

1 Dry-fry the chiles in a frying pan or griddle until the skins are scorched. Alternatively, spear them on a long-handled metal skewer and roast them over the flame of a gas burner until the skins blister and darken. Do not let the flesh burn.

2 Place the roasted chiles in a strong plastic bag and tie the top to keep the steam in. Set aside for 20 minutes.

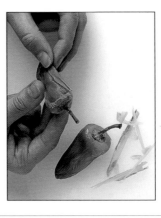

3 Remove the chiles from the bag and peel off the skins. Cut off the stems, then slit the chiles and scrape out the seeds.

Above: Fresno chiles

and 2¾ inches wide, and are sometimes said to be heart-shaped. Although not very hot, poblanos have a rich, earthy flavor which is intensified when the chiles are roasted and peeled. They are widely used in Mexican cooking, notably in Stuffed Chiles (*Chiles Rellenos*). Anaheim chiles, which are widely available in the United States and sometimes in the United Kingdom, can be substituted for poblanos.

Fresno Heat level 8. Looking much like elongated sweet peppers, fresnos are about 2½ inches long and ¾ inch wide. They have a hot, sweet flavor and are used in salsas, as well as in meat, fish and vegetable dishes. They are particularly good in Black Bean Salsa and Guacamole.

Buying and Storing Fresh Chiles

Look for firm fresh chiles, with shiny skins. Try to avoid any specimens that are dull or limp, as they will be past their prime. Fresh chiles can be successfully stored in a plastic bag in the refrigerator for up to 3 weeks. If they are to be chopped and added to cooked dishes, they can be seeded, chopped and then frozen, ready for use until needed.

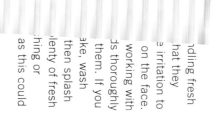

ndling fresh
hat they
e irritation to
on the face.
working with
ds thoroughly
them. If you
ake, wash
then splash
lenty of fresh
hing or
as this could

3 Carefully scrape out all of the seeds and remove the core with a small sharp knife.

rmly at the stem
gthwise with a

4 Cut out any white membrane from the inside of the chiles. Keep the knife close to the flesh so that all the membrane is removed.

from both halves
ing a thin slice of
e as you do so.
se the white
ake it easier to

5 At this point make sure you carefully discard all of the seeds and membrane that are now lying on the board. Then take each half chile and cut as required. To chop finely first cut the chile half into thin strips. Then bunch the strips together and cut across them to produce tiny pieces. If the chile is being added to a dish that will be cooked for some time you can chop it less finely.

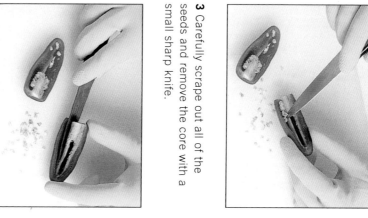

Ingredients 47

DRIED CHILES

Dried chiles are nothing new. The convenience of a product that could be stored and rehydrated when needed was realized centuries ago. Chiles were originally sun-dried, but today are more likely to be dried in an oven. Either way, they are a valuable ingredient, and are extensively used in this book because they are so much easier to obtain than fresh chiles.

In many cases, drying intensifies the flavor of chiles. Depending on the process used, drying can also impart extra flavor, as when jalapeños are dried and smoked. Not only does the flavor deepen to a rich smokiness, but the name of the chile changes, and it becomes a chipotle. The fact that the same chile can have two names, depending on whether it is fresh or dried, can be confusing, and it may be simpler to think of dried chiles as separate varieties.

The heat rating given for the dried chiles in the list that follows is based on the same scale as that used for the fresh chiles on the previous pages.

Drying seems to spread the capsaicin through the chiles, so removing the seeds and membrane will do little to alter their heat. The seeds of a dried chile add very little to the flavor, however, so if they are loose, discard them. Dried chiles can be ground into a powder or cut into strips before being used. Unless the chiles are to be added to a dish with a high proportion of liquid, they are usually soaked in water before use.

Buying and Storing Dried Chiles

Good quality dried chiles should be flexible, not brittle. Store them in an airtight jar in a cool, dry place. For short term storage, the refrigerator is ideal, although they can also be frozen. Do not keep dried chiles for more than a year or the flavor may fade.

The following is a list of some of the more common dried chiles, all of which feature in this book.

Ancho Heat scale 3. The most common dried chile in Mexico, the ancho is a dried red poblano chile, and has a fruity, slightly sharp flavor. When rehydrated, anchos can be used to make Stuffed Chiles (*Chiles Rellenos*), but should not be peeled first.

Cascabel Heat scale 4. The name means "little rattle" and refers to the noise that the seeds make inside the chile. This chile has a chocolate brown skin, and

Below: Cascabel chiles

Above: Chile powder

Above: Ancho chiles

Grinding Chiles

This method gives a distinctive and smoky taste to the resulting powdered chile.

1 Soak the chiles, pat dry and then dry-fry in a heavy pan until crisp.

2 Transfer to a mortar and grind into a fine powder with a pestle. Store in an airtight container.

remains dark, even after soaking. Cascabels have a slightly nutty flavor and are often added to salsas such as *tomate verde*.

Chipotle Heat scale 6. These are smoked jalapeños. They add a

Right: Chipotle chiles

wonderfully rich smoky flavor to all sorts of dishes, from barbecue sauces to chicken, and are great in cowboy-style beans with pork. One of the simplest ways of using chipotles is to purée the soaked chiles, then stir them into cream to make a rich dipping sauce.

Guajillo Heat scale 3. Another popular dried chile in Mexican cuisine, the guajillo is used in sauces or

Above: Pasilla chiles

Right: Pasada chiles

Above: Guajillo chiles

Above: Habañero chiles

st

ong and

has a

skin. A

guajillos is

eading on

ng.

e 10. This is

m all, a chile

puréed,

he blender

tern-shaped,

and

o called

are often

hili sauces.

s chile is

citrus and

ed in soups

or cooking

la means

dried version

the chilaca.

1 inch wide,

and is suitable

r suggests

ground and

e chile is used

uding *moles*.

smoked

liar to the

Soaking Dried Chiles

In order to appreciate their full flavor, it is recommended that dried chiles that are not being ground should be soaked before being used. The amount of time chiles need to rehydrate depends on the type, the thickness of the skin and how dry they are. The longer they soak the better, so if there is time, leave them in the water for 1 hour before cooking.

1 Wipe them to remove any dirt, and brush away any seeds that are accessible.

2 Soak the dried chiles in a bowl of hot water for about 10 minutes (longer if possible) until the color is restored and the chile has swelled and softened.

3 Drain, cut off the stems, then slit the chiles and scrape out the seeds with a small sharp knife. Slice or chop the flesh. If the chiles are to be puréed, put them in a blender or food processor with a little of the soaking water and process them until smooth.

VEGETABLES

Mexico's indigenous peoples were very good agriculturists, and when the Spanish invaded they found a country blessed with abundant vegetables, including corn, sweet potatoes, *jicama*, pumpkins and zucchini. The Spanish in turn introduced onions, garlic, green beans, cabbage and cauliflower, all of which were integrated into the Mexican cuisine.

CORN

The vegetable we know as corn has been grown in the Americas for over five thousand years. It was brought to Europe by the Spanish in the late 15th century, but long before that it was a staple food of the indigenous peoples of Mexico, who used every part of the corn, including the husks and silks.

Description

An ear of corn consists of yellow, plump kernels on a firm cob, sheathed in long green leaves or husks. Between the leaves and the kernels are long thin threads called silks. Mexicans traditionally use these for tying *tamales*, but elsewhere they are usually discarded.

Buying and Storing

Look for ears whose outer leaves are a fresh, tender green. They should not be limp or faded. One way of testing whether the corn is fresh is to squeeze one of the kernels gently. A milky liquid should ooze out. Corn should be cooked within 24 hours of being purchased, because the sugar starts turning to starch the moment it is cut. The older the corn, the less sweet it will be.

Preparation

Peel off the husks, then pull off the silks. (If necessary, scrub the ears with a vegetable brush to remove any remaining silks.) If the corn is to be cooked on the grill, the husks can be pulled back, then replaced after removing the silks.

Main Uses and Cooking Tips

Corn can be cooked in boiling water, but do not add salt or the kernels will toughen. They can also be cooked in the oven or on a grill. In Mexico, corn is a popular street food. The cooked ears are dipped in cream, then sprinkled with cheese. A similar dish involves removing the kernels from the ears and cooking them in cream with pickled jalapeños and cheese.

Above: Beans

GREEN BEANS

Green beans have been growing in the Americas for hundreds of years. In Mexico, lima beans, sometimes mistakenly called fava beans, are widely used, as are string beans.

Buying and Storing

Pods should be bright and crisp. Use on the day bought if possible.

Preparation

Trim the beans (cut off both ends) and remove any strings on the sides of the pods. Lima beans and fava beans must be removed from their pods before use, and are sometimes blanched.

Main Uses and Cooking Tips

Mexicans use beans in salads and vegetable dishes. A favorite dish is lima beans with a tomato sauce. Beans are best cooked briefly in boiling water or steamed until they are tender. Both these methods ensure that the beans retain maximum color, texture and flavor.

Above: Corn

Right: Sweet potatoes

SWEET POTATOES

One of the staple foods of the indigenous peoples of Mexico in pre-Columbian times, sweet potatoes are still a very important food.

Description and Varieties

Sweet potatoes are starchy tubers, and need to be cooked before being eaten. There are many different varieties, ranging from pale-skinned sweet potatoes with pale crumbly flesh to darker tubers with thick skins and moist flesh. The skin color can range from pink to deep purple, and the flesh can range from creamy white to the more familiar vivid orange. As their name suggests, they have a sweet flavor, but with a hint of spice.

Buying and Storing

Sweet potatoes have smooth skins and should not be damaged or soft. Smaller specimens often have finer flavor than large ones. They can be stored in a cool, dark place for up to 1 week.

Preparation

Cook sweet potatoes in their

Tips

Sw... both sweet
an...oked slowly
in...boiled. Try
the...th a little
bu...e nutmeg,
sa...ned
pc...chiles, are
a...t to grilled
fo...es are
ex...ney are also
us...s.

v: Jicamas

JICAMAS

The *jicama*—or yam bean—is a native of Central America. It was introduced to the Philippines by the Spanish, and from there it spread to China, where it is still popular today. In fact, Chinese supermarkets are a good source of *jicama*. The Chinese name for it is *saa got*, but you may also find it labeled Chinese turnip.

Description

Jicama is the root of a climbing bean plant. The young beans are edible, but older ones are poisonous. It looks like a turnip or beet, but has a conical base. The skin is light brown and quite thin. The moist, creamy-colored flesh tastes slightly fruity, and the texture resembles that of a crisp green apple or a water chestnut. *Jicama* can be eaten raw or cooked.

Buying and Storing

Look for firm *jicamas* that are about the size of a large turnip; larger ones may be a bit woody. To keep the crisp texture, store them in the refrigerator for up to 1 week.

Preparation

Peel off the thin, papery skin by hand or with a sharp knife, then slice the *jicama* thinly.

Main Uses and Cooking Tips

Raw *jicama* makes a refreshing snack when it is sprinkled with freshly squeezed orange juice and served with chili powder and salt. It is also delicious added to salads and used in salsas. *Jicama* retains its pleasingly crisp texture when boiled, as long as it is not overcooked. Mexicans sometimes like to use grated *jicama* in desserts.

SQUASH

Pumpkins and other types of squash, cucumbers and *chayotes* all belong to the same family, and have been cultivated since ancient times. Pumpkin seeds dating back as far as 7000 B.C. have been found in Mexico. The word "squash" comes from an Indian word, "askutasquash," meaning raw or uncooked, which may seem odd to those of us accustomed to eating squash cooked. However, there are numerous types of squash, and some are indeed delicious eaten raw.

Description

There are two main classifications of squash—summer and winter. Many of the summer squash are now available all year round, but it can still be useful to differentiate between the two distinct groups.

Summer squash grow on bushes and have thin, edible skins and soft seeds. Examples include zucchini, patty pans and yellow squash. The flesh is soft,

Above: Summer squash

generally pale in color and has a high water content. It only needs a little cooking, and has a mild flavor. The seeds are dispersed through the flesh, and are usually eaten with it. Zucchini can be eaten raw, in salads. Winter squash have harder, thicker skins and tough seeds. They may grow on bushes, but are often the fruit of vine plants. The skin is usually cut off and discarded, although if the squash is roasted, its skin may be soft enough to eat. Acorn, butternut, spaghetti, onion squash and pumpkin are some of the better known varieties. The flesh is often yellow or deep orange, is firmer and requires longer cooking than that of summer squash. The seeds are generally removed and discarded before cooking, although some,

such as pumpkin seeds, are a valuable food in their own right.

The blossoms or flowers from both winter and summer squash are edible, and there are a number of Mexican recipes for cooking squash blossoms. In Mexico you can buy the blossoms separately, and they are sold at some specialty food stores elsewhere, but most cooks who want to try them will have to harvest them from home-grown vegetables. They are delicious coated in light batter and fried.

Buying and Storing

Summer squash, and zucchini in particular, are best when they are small, slim and still tender. They should have bright, smooth, unblemished skins with no bruising. They should be stored in the refrigerator, and will only keep for 3–4 days. The thicker skins of winter squash make them much better for long term keeping. They can be stored in a cool room for up to 1 month, depending on how mature they were when picked and on how old they were when sold. When buying winter squash, choose specimens that are heavy for their size and that have unmarked skins.

Above: Pumpkin

Main Uses and Cooking Tips

Summer squash can be steamed, stir-fried, boiled, baked or even coated in batter and deep-fried. As the flesh is soft, it will need to be cooked for only a few minutes and should still retain some bite. Popular Mexican recipes include Zucchini Torte and Zucchini with Cheese and Green Chiles.

Winter squash are often cut into pieces, seeded and baked, steamed or boiled. They need to be cooked for longer than summer squash because the flesh is firmer. The skin is usually discarded, and this can be done either before cooking or after.

Mexicans often roast pumpkins in large chunks. They also cook pumpkin in water and sugar, as a dessert, or bake it with sugar and spices. Other types of squash are used in similar ways, and cooked squash often features

Winter squash

Inside is a
appearance to
ayote seeds
flesh is pale
rt green apple

th a smooth,
that is free
mishes or
uising. Smaller

chayotes will be more flavorful than large ones. They keep well in the refrigerator and can be stored for up to 1 month.

Main Uses and Cooking Tips

Chayotes have a fairly mild flavor and are best peeled and served simply in salads or salsas, with a squeeze of lime or orange juice and some chiles. If they are cooked, they should be seasoned well. The mild flavor makes them ideal for combining with other, more strongly flavored ingredients. To cook *chayotes*, either peel and cook them in the same way as summer squash, or bake them.

Left: Chayote

Baked Chayote

Cut them in half, brush the cut sides with oil, then either fill them with a vegetable stuffing or simply sprinkle them with salt, pepper and a little spice, if desired. Bake in a pre-heated oven at 375°F for 25 minutes or until tender all the way through when pierced with a skewer.

ALCOHOLIC DRINKS

Mexico has a large number of fermented beverages, mainly derived from fruit or a plant called the agave. Many of these are an acquired taste and not particularly popular outside the country.

BEER

Mexicans were introduced to the brewing process by the German settlers who came to their country, and many of the brewing companies in existence today have German roots. Mexican beer production centers largely around the north of the country, although there are breweries everywhere. The city of Monterrey in Nuevo León is renowned as the beer capital of Mexico. Many people are employed in brewing and subsidiary industries such as glass making, carton manufacturing and label printing,

Above: Beers

and the beer industry is an important part of the economy. Mexican beer brands such as Dos Equis, Sol and Corona are exported, although these are often brewed outside Mexico on licence. Other brands, such as Tecate, which are less readily available, are worth trying.

WINE

Wine production on a large scale was actively discouraged during the years of Spanish rule, as the conquerors wanted to promote wines and spirits from Spain. A wine industry finally did grow up, however, in Baja California, and even today, the major vineyards are in the northwest of the country, although there is some wine production further south. New World wines have become an important part of the wine market in recent years, and there is increased interest in wines from Mexico, which are very reasonably priced. The popular grapes for the production of white wine are Chardonnay, Sauvignon Blanc,

Left: Red wine

Right: White wine

Riesling and Chenin Blanc, while established red grape varieties include Cabernet Sauvignon, Pinot Noir and Grenache, as well as Merlot.

PULQUE

Records from the time of Cortés make reference to *pulque* being drunk by the Aztecs. It is a beer-like drink made from the sap of the agave plant, which is commonly called *maguey* in Mexico. While chocolate drinks were the preserve of the ruling classes in 16th century Mexico, *pulque* was drunk by the common people. The drink is still popular today, and *pulquerías*, small bars selling *pulque* are widespread. These bars were once reputed to be wild, dangerous places, and children and people in uniform were not allowed to frequent them.

The traditional method for making *pulque* has changed little since the days of the Aztecs. The sap is extracted from the plant, allowed to ferment for a few weeks, then drunk. If left, it would continue to ferment and would quite soon become undrinkable. The short life span of the product means that it is seldom sold outside Mexico.

Pulque, which is between 6 and 8 percent proof, has a unique, slightly earthy flavor, and is very definitely an acquired taste. In Mexico, efforts to make it more universally acceptable include blending it with a fruit juice such as pineapple and selling it in cans.

Right: Pulque

Left: Kahlúa

KAHLÚA

This ... in Mexico city a... le world. It is a... make after- ... es in dinne... when cock... lass with um floated drunk... also blended eam.

c name ...quila, ...ussed in ...s just ...western *mescal* ... the *maguey* This ...mental drinki...s

competed to see who would land the worm, and the reputation of *mescal* suffered in the process. For the record, the worm was originally placed in the bottle to demonstrate the alcoholic proof of the *mescal*, the argument being that the preservation of the worm (actually a moth larva) proved the potency of the alcohol.

Oaxaca is largely credited by aficionados as being one of the best areas for *mescal* production. The traditional way of producing the spirit involves taking the heart or *piña* from a number of plants and cooking them in a large pit. An average *piña* will weigh about 110 pounds. The procedure begins with the digging of the pit. A large fire is built in the bottom, and a layer of rocks is piled on top. When the fire has been burning under the rocks for about a day, the *piñas* are added. They are left to cook for 2–3 days. The cooking plays a large part in determining the flavor, aroma and smoothness of the *mescal*, and is a skilled job. After cooking, the *piñas* are removed from the pit and crushed to release the juice. This, together with the fibrous part of the plant, is mixed with water and left to ferment. More modern methods, involving special ovens, are now used by commercial producers to cook the *piñas* and control the all-important fermentation process.

TEQUILA

Tequila is, without doubt, the Mexican spirit which is best known outside the country. A specific type of *mescal*, it is becoming steadily more popular, especially among younger drinkers.

The Spanish taught Mexicans the art of distilling. *Pulque*, the national drink made from the agave plant, was the perfect subject, and they began by distilling it to make *mescal*. This was then distilled a second time to produce tequila. If *mescal* is brandy, then tequila is Cognac, and is subject to similar

controls to those that are imposed by the French government on their famous spirit. There are also parallels with the production of Champagne, in that tequila production is tightly regulated and may only take place in specially designated areas.

Tequila takes its name from the eponymous town in Jalisco where it was first made. The name means "volcano" in the local Indian dialect. Jalisco is also the home of *mariachi* music, which possibly explains how tequila gained its image as a fun, party drink.

Production

Tequila is made from the sap of the blue agave plant, which is not a cactus, as is commonly believed, but is related to the amaryllis. The leaves of each plant are cut off to leave the *piña*,

which is then steam cooked. The juice is fermented, then distilled twice, the second time in a copper still, after which it is bottled or matured in casks. All aspects of the process are rigidly controlled and documented.

Flavor Variations

There are several different types of tequila, and innumerable brands of all of these. Each brand has a different flavor, determined by the soil and the climate where the agave was grown, the amount of sugar the agave contained and the finer details of the processing, including the cooking of the *piña* and the fermentation of the juice. Some tequilas are aged in casks, and the type of wood used, together with the duration of the aging process, will also influence the flavor of the finished product.

Not all tequilas are 100 percent agave spirit; some are blended with cane spirit, but by law tequila must contain at least 51 percent agave spirit. Blended tequilas are becoming less popular in foreign markets as consumers become more discriminating. At one time

Below: Tequila and lime

Left: Tequila blanco

Left: Mescal

Right: Tequila

you could walk into a bar in Britain or Europe and find only one type of tequila—and that was primarily used for making margaritas. However, the increasing popularity of Mexican food has led to a gradual rise in the popularity of tequila and a greater appreciation of the various types, and in some places today there are even specialty tequila bars, which stock a vast range of different types and brands of this exciting spirit.

Left: Margarita

Tequi...

Drink
the c...
of sa...
wedg...
the b...
drink
origin...
the s...
salt a...
neces...
famil...
stanc...

...r Tequila

...ome a
...a drinker
...erent
...lies,
...eans are
...orings
...d syrups

Right: A bottle of Tequila anejo

Typ...

Jov...
...een bottled
imr...
It is
usu...
mes be
gol...
ation also
incl...
...een aged
for...

Rep...
...color and
has
...months.
It h...
than joven

...aged in
...e and has

...given to
...la that
...vored.

triple sec—orange liqueur—is added. A margarita may be served neat, as it comes out of the bottle, or over ice cubes, or "frozen" with crushed ice.

In Mexico, tequila is often sipped alternately with a glass of sangrita, a tomato juice flavored with chiles and other seasonings. When the tequila and tomato juice are combined, the drink becomes a Bloody Maria.

Below: Two types of Curados; bottles of blanco tequila that have had flavoring added. Here a few red chiles have been added to the bottle on the left, and three vanilla pods to the one on the right. The tequila will take on the flavor of the chile or vanilla in just a few days.

RECIPES

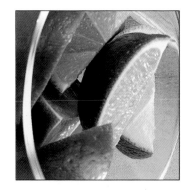

so much more than enchiladas and empanadas,

oth worthy of mention. Until relatively recently,

restaurants outside the country tended to serve

which owed its origins to Mexico but had been

country's northern neighbors. Today, discerning

laces that serve true Mexican food—colorful,

ot always fiery—and are eager to recreate their

favorite dishes at home.

ourmet stores and mail-order suppliers have

rging market by stocking specialty ingredients—

tens as tomatillos and the less common varieties

has made it much easier for enthusiastic cooks.

w are a cross-section of all the different regional

this exciting country and illustrate the diversity

nd cooking methods that make Mexican cooking

so fascinating and delicious.

SALSAS

Salsa simply means sauce, and ... refreshing, cooked or fresh, all ar... are served as relishes. There ... the cooked sauces is Pum... a rich ...

...ome of the finest. Hot and spicy, cool and ...are varied. Some are poured onto food, others ...ssic salsas that are widely used. Chief among ...Pepián, in which the seeds are roasted to give ...n Tomatillo Sauce, known as Salsa Verde, is ...ben served over enchiladas or with pork. ...ncooked sauces, Classic Tomato Salsa, known ...nchera, or Salsa Mexicana, is probably the ...ular. This combination of tomatoes, onion, ...d lime makes a superb accompaniment that ...lmost every table. Unlike commercial sauces, ...alsas contain neither oil nor added sugar, but ...r on fresh raw fruits and vegetables, making ...lent choice for the health-conscious. ...s, incomparable flavors and adaptability of ...m indispensable to any good cook, and their ...ress extends far beyond the boundaries of ...Mexican cuisine.

CLASSIC TOMATO SALSA

This is the traditional tomato-based salsa that most people associate with Mexican food. There are innumerable recipes for it, but the basics of onion, tomato, chile and cilantro are common to every one of them. Serve this salsa as a condiment with a wide variety of dishes.

SERVES SIX AS AN ACCOMPANIMENT

INGREDIENTS

3–6 fresh serrano chiles
1 large white onion
grated zest and juice of 2 limes, plus
   strips of lime zest, to garnish
8 ripe, firm tomatoes
large bunch of cilantro
¼ teaspoon sugar
salt

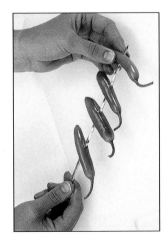

1 Use three chiles for a salsa of medium heat, up to six if you like it hot. To peel the chiles, spear them on a long-handled metal skewer and roast them over the flame of a gas burner until the skins blister and darken. Do not let the flesh burn. Alternatively, dry-fry them in a griddle until the skins are scorched.

2 Place the roasted chiles in a strong plastic bag and tie the top of the bag to keep the steam in. Set aside for about 20 minutes.

3 Meanwhile, chop the onion finely and put it in a bowl with the lime rind and juice. The lime juice will soften the onion.

4 Remove the chiles from the bag and peel off the skins. Cut off the stalks, then slit the chiles and scrape out the seeds with a sharp knife. Chop the flesh roughly and set aside.

5 Cut a small cross in the bottom of each tomato. Place the tomatoes in a heatproof bowl and pour in boiling water to cover.

6 Leave the tomatoes in the water for 3 minutes, then lift them out using a slotted spoon and plunge them into a bowl of cold water. Drain. The skins will have begun to peel back from the crosses. Remove the skins completely.

VARIATIONS
Use scallions or mild red onions instead of white onion. For a smoky flavor, use chipotle chiles instead of fresh serrano chiles.

7 Dice the peeled tomatoes and put them in a bowl. Add the chopped onion which should have softened, together with the lime mixture. Chop the cilantro finely.

8 Add the cilantro to the salsa, with the chiles and the sugar. Mix gently until the sugar has dissolved and all the ingredients are coated in lime juice. Cover and chill for 2–3 hours to let the flavors blend. The salsa will keep for 3–4 days in the refrigerator. Garnish with the strips of lime zest just before serving.

GREEN TOMATILLO SAUCE

THIS SAUCE, WITH ITS DISTINCTIVE GREEN COLOR AND SHARP TASTE, IS A POPULAR CHOICE FOR POURING ONTO ENCHILADAS. WHEN THE CREAM IS ADDED, IT IS PERFECT FOR POACHED FISH OR WITH CHICKEN BREASTS. FRESH TOMATILLOS ARE DIFFICULT TO OBTAIN OUTSIDE MEXICO, BUT THE SAUCE CAN BE MADE WITH CANNED TOMATILLOS. INSTRUCTIONS FOR BOTH VERSIONS ARE GIVEN HERE.

SERVES FOUR AS A SAUCE
FOR A MAIN COURSE

INGREDIENTS
11 ounces fresh tomatillos,
plus ½ cup stock or water **or**
11 ounces drained canned
tomatillos, plus ¼ cup stock
or water
2 fresh serrano chiles
4 garlic cloves, crushed
1 tablespoon vegetable oil
small bunch of cilantro
½ cup heavy cream
(optional)
salt

1 If using fresh tomatillos, remove the husks and cut the tomatillos into quarters. Place them in a saucepan and add the stock or water. Cook over medium heat for 8–10 minutes, until the flesh is soft and transparent.

2 Remove the stems from the chiles, slit them and scrape out the seeds with a small knife. Chop the flesh roughly and place it in a food processor or blender with the garlic.

3 Add the tomatillos to the processor or blender with their cooking liquid and process for a few minutes until almost smooth. If using drained canned tomatillos, simply quarter and put in the blender or food processor with the smaller amount of stock or water and the chopped chiles and garlic. Process until almost smooth.

4 Heat the oil in a heavy frying pan and add the processed tomatillo purée. Reduce the heat and cook gently, stirring, for about 5 minutes, until the sauce thickens. Be sure to keep stirring the sauce all the time, since it can easily stick and burn.

5 Chop the cilantro and add it to the sauce, with salt to taste. Cook for a few minutes, stirring occasionally.

6 Stir in the cream, if using, and warm the sauce through. Do not let it boil after adding the cream. Serve immediately.

GUACAMOLE

ONE OF THE BEST LOVED MEXICAN ⟨⟩ OF CREAMY AVOCADO, TOMATOES, CHILES,
CILANTRO AND LIME NOW APPEARS ⟨⟩ THE WORLD. PURCHASED GUACAMOLE
USUALLY CONTAINS MAYONNAISE, W⟨⟩ ⟨⟩RVE THE AVOCADO, BUT THIS IS NOT AN
INGREDIENT IN TRADITIONAL RECIP⟨⟩.

SERVES SIX TO EIGHT

INGREDIENTS
4 medium tomatoes
4 ripe avocados
juice of 1 lime
½ small onion
2 garlic cloves
small bunch of cilantro,
chopped
3 fresh red fresno chiles
salt
tortilla chips, to serve

1 Cut a cross in the bottom of each tomato. Place the tomatoes in a heatproof bowl and pour in boiling water to cover.

2 Leave the tomatoes in the water for 3 minutes, then lift them out using a slotted spoon and plunge them into a bowl of cold water. Drain. The skins will have begun to peel back from the crosses. Remove the skins completely. Cut the tomatoes in half, remove the seeds with a teaspoon, then chop the flesh roughly and set it aside.

COOK'S TIP
Smooth-skinned fuerte avocados are native to Mexico, so would be ideal for this dip. If they are not available, use any avocados, but make sure they are ripe. To test, gently press the top of the avocado; it should give a little.

4 Chop the onion finely, then crush the garlic. Add both to the avocado and mix well. Stir in the cilantro.

5 Remove the stems from the chiles, slit them and scrape out the seeds with a small sharp knife. Chop the chiles finely and add them to the avocado mixture, with the chopped tomatoes. Mix well.

⟨⟩f, then remove
⟨⟩ut of the
⟨⟩od processor
almost smooth,
⟨⟩nd stir in the

6 Check the seasoning and add salt to taste. Cover closely with plastic wrap or a tight-fitting lid and chill for 1 hour before serving as a dip with tortilla chips. If it is well covered, guacamole will keep in the refrigerator for 2–3 days.

BLACK BEAN SALSA

THIS SALSA HAS A VERY STRIKING APPEARANCE. IT IS RARE TO FIND A BLACK SAUCE, AND IT PROVIDES A WONDERFUL CONTRAST TO THE MORE COMMON REDS AND GREENS ON THE PLATE. THE PASADO CHILES ADD A SUBTLE CITRUS FLAVOR. USE THE SALSA A DAY OR TWO AFTER MAKING TO LET THE FLAVORS DEVELOP FULLY.

SERVES FOUR AS AN ACCOMPANIMENT

INGREDIENTS

generous ½ cup black beans,
  soaked overnight in water
  to cover
1 pasado chile
2 fresh red fresno chiles
1 red onion
grated zest and juice of 1 lime
2 tablespoons Mexican beer
  (optional)
1 tablespoon olive oil
small bunch of cilantro, chopped
salt

1 Drain the beans and put them in a large saucepan. Pour in water to cover and place the lid on the pan. Bring to a boil, lower the heat slightly and simmer the beans for about 40 minutes or until tender. They should still have a little bite and should not have begun to disintegrate. Drain, rinse under cold water, then drain again and leave the beans until cold.

2 Soak the pasado chile in hot water for about 10 minutes, until softened. Drain, remove the stalk, then slit the chile and scrape out the seeds with a small sharp knife. Chop the flesh finely.

COOK'S TIP
Mexican beer is a lager-type beer. Few brands are to be found in this country, but the most popular, *Dos Equis* (Double X), is readily available.

3 Spear the fresno chiles on a long-handled metal skewer and roast them over the flame of a gas burner until the skins blister and darken. Do not let the flesh burn. Alternatively, dry-fry them on a griddle until the skins are scorched. Then place the roasted chiles in a strong plastic bag and tie the top to keep the steam in. Set aside for 20 minutes.

4 Meanwhile, chop the red onion finely. Remove the chiles from the bag and peel off the skins. Slit them, remove the seeds and chop them finely.

5 Transfer the beans to a bowl and add the onion and both types of chile. Stir in the lime zest and juice, beer, oil and cilantro. Season with salt and mix well. Chill before serving.

PINTO BEAN SA

THESE BEANS HAVE A PRETTY, SPECK   HE SMOKY FLAVOR OF THE
CHIPOTLE CHILES AND THE HERBAL   A CHILE CONTRAST WELL
WITH THE TART TOMATILLOS.

SERVES FOUR AS AN ACCOMPANIMENT

INGREDIENTS

generous ½ cup pinto beans,
soaked overnight in water
to cover
2 chipotle chiles
1 pasilla chile
2 garlic cloves, peeled
½ onion
7 ounces fresh tomatillos
salt

| put them in a
in water to cover
ne pan. Bring to a
ghtly and simmer
ninutes or until
ave begun to
nse under cold
in and transfer
e beans until cold.

1 be substituted,
resh flavor, add a

4 Chop the onion and tomatillos and stir
them into the beans. Add the chile
paste and mix well. Add salt to taste,
cover and chill before serving.

3 Roast the garlic in a dry frying pan
over medium heat for a few minutes,
until the cloves start to turn golden.
Crush them and add them to the beans.

2 Soak the chipotle and pasilla chiles
in hot water for about 10 minutes, until
softened. Drain, reserving the soaking
water. Remove the stems, then slit each
chile and scrape out the seeds with a
small sharp knife. Chop the flesh finely
and mix into a smooth paste with a little
of the soaking water.

CHIPOTLE SAUCE

THE SMOKY FLAVOR OF THIS SAUCE MAKES IT IDEAL FOR GRILLED FOOD, EITHER AS A MARINADE OR AS AN ACCOMPANIMENT. IT IS ALSO WONDERFUL STIRRED INTO CREAM CHEESE AS A SANDWICH FILLING WITH CHICKEN. CHIPOTLE CHILES ARE SMOKED DRIED JALAPEÑO CHILES.

SERVES SIX AS AN ACCOMPANIMENT

INGREDIENTS
1¼ pounds tomatoes
5 chipotle chiles
3 garlic cloves, roughly chopped
⅔ cup red wine
1 teaspoon dried oregano
4 tablespoons honey
1 teaspoon American mustard
½ teaspoon ground black pepper
salt

1 Preheat the oven to 400°F. Cut the tomatoes into quarters and place them in a roasting pan. Roast for 45 minutes–1 hour, until they are charred and softened.

2 Meanwhile, soak the chiles in a bowl of cold water to cover for about 20 minutes or until soft. Remove the stalks, slit the chiles and scrape out the seeds with a small sharp knife. Chop the flesh roughly.

3 Remove the tomatoes from the oven, let them cool slightly, then remove the skins. If you prefer a smooth sauce, remove the seeds. Chop the tomatoes and put them in a blender or food processor. Add the chopped chiles and garlic with the red wine. Process until smooth, then add the oregano, honey, mustard and black pepper. Process briefly to mix, then taste and season with salt.

4 Scrape the mixture into a small saucepan. Place over medium heat and stir until the mixture boils. Lower the heat and simmer the sauce for about 10 minutes, stirring occasionally, until it has reduced and thickened. Spoon into a bowl and serve hot or cold.

GUAJILLO CHILI SAUCE

THIS SAUCE CAN BE SERVED OVER ENCHILADAS OR STEAMED VEGETABLES. IT IS ALSO GOOD WITH MEATS, SUCH AS PORK, AND A LITTLE MAKES A FINE SEASONING FOR SOUPS OR STEWS. MADE FROM DRIED CHILES, IT HAS A WELL ROUNDED, FRUITY FLAVOR AND IS NOT TOO HOT.

SERVES FOUR AS AN ACCOMPANIMENT

INGREDIENTS
2 tomatoes, total weight about 7 ounces
2 red bell peppers, cored, seeded and quartered
3 garlic cloves, in their skins
2 ancho chiles
2 guajillo chiles
2 tablespoons tomato paste
1 teaspoon dried oregano
1 teaspoon dark brown sugar
1¼ cups chicken stock

1 Preheat the oven to 400°F. Cut the tomatoes into quarters and place them in a roasting pan with the peppers and whole garlic cloves. Roast for 45 minutes–1 hour, until the tomatoes and peppers are slightly charred and the garlic has softened.

2 Put the peppers in a strong plastic bag and tie the top to keep the steam in. Set aside for 20 minutes. Remove the skin from the tomatoes. Meanwhile, soak the chiles in boiling water for 15 minutes, until soft.

3 Remove the peppers from the bag and rub off the skins. Cut them in half, remove the cores and seeds, then chop the flesh roughly and put it in a food processor or blender. Drain the chiles, remove the stems, then slit them and scrape out the seeds with a sharp knife. Chop the chiles roughly and add them to the peppers.

4 Add the roasted tomatoes to the food processor or blender. Squeeze the roasted garlic out of the skins and add to the tomato mixture, with the tomato paste, oregano, brown sugar and stock. Process until smooth.

5 Pour the mixture into a saucepan, place over medium heat and bring to a boil. Lower the heat and simmer for 10–15 minutes, until the sauce has reduced to about half. Transfer to a bowl and serve immediately or, if serving cold, cover, let cool, then chill until needed. The sauce will keep in the refrigerator for up to a week.

ROASTED TOMATO SALSA

SLOW ROASTING THESE TOMATOES TO A SEMI-DRIED STATE RESULTS IN A VERY RICH, FULL-FLAVORED SWEET SAUCE. THE COSTEÑO AMARILLO CHILE IS MILD AND HAS A FRESH LIGHT FLAVOR, MAKING IT THE PERFECT PARTNER FOR THE RICH TOMATO TASTE. THIS SALSA IS GREAT WITH TUNA OR SEA BASS AND MAKES A GREAT SANDWICH FILLING WHEN TEAMED WITH CREAMY CHEESE.

SERVES SIX AS AN ACCOMPANIMENT

INGREDIENTS

1¼ pounds tomatoes
8 small shallots
5 garlic cloves
sea salt
1 fresh rosemary sprig
2 costeño amarillo chiles
grated zest and juice of ½ small lemon
2 tablespoons extra virgin olive oil
¼ teaspoon dark brown sugar

1 Preheat the oven to 325°F. Cut the tomatoes into quarters and place them on a baking tray.

2 Peel the shallots and garlic and add them to the roasting pan. Sprinkle with sea salt. Roast for 1¼ hours or until the tomatoes are beginning to dry. Do not let them burn or blacken or they will have a bitter taste.

3 Let the tomatoes cool, then peel off the skins and chop the flesh finely. Place in a bowl. Remove the outer layer of skin from any shallots that have toughened.

4 Using a large, sharp knife, chop the shallots and garlic roughly, place them with the tomatoes in a bowl and mix.

5 Strip the rosemary leaves from the woody stem and chop them finely. Add half to the tomato and shallot mixture and mix lightly.

6 Soak the chiles in hot water for about 10 minutes, until soft. Drain, remove the stems, slit them and scrape out the seeds with a sharp knife. Chop the flesh finely and add it to the tomato mixture.

7 Stir in the lemon zest and juice, the olive oil and the sugar. Mix well, taste and add more salt if needed. Cover and chill for at least an hour before serving, sprinkled with the remaining rosemary. It will keep for up to a week in the refrigerator.

COOK'S TIP
Use plum tomatoes or vine tomatoes, which have more flavor than tomatoes that have been grown for their keeping properties rather than their flavor. Cherry tomatoes make delicious roast tomato salsa, and there is no need to peel them after roasting.

JICAMA SALSA

THE JICAMA IS A ROUND, BROWN ROOT VEGETABLE WITH A TEXTURE SOMEWHERE BETWEEN THAT OF A WATER CHESTNUT AND A CRISP APPLE. IT CAN BE EATEN RAW OR COOKED, AND IS ALWAYS PEELED. LOOK FOR JICAMAS AT ETHNIC FOOD STORES.

SERVES FOUR AS AN ACCOMPANIMENT

INGREDIENTS
1 small red onion
juice of 2 limes
3 small oranges
1 *jicama*, about 1 pound
½ cucumber
1 fresh red fresno chile

1 Cut the onion in half, then slice each half finely. Place in a bowl, add the lime juice and let soak while you prepare the remaining ingredients.

2 Slice the top and bottom off each orange. Stand an orange on a board, then carefully slice off all the peel and pith. Hold the orange over a bowl and cut carefully between the membranes so that the segments fall into the bowl. Having cut out all the segments, squeeze the pulp over the bowl to extract the remaining juice.

3 Peel the *jicama* and rinse it in cold water. Cut it into quarters, then slice finely. Add to the bowl of orange juice.

COOK'S TIP
The juices of citrus fruits are very useful in preserving color and freshness, and add more than flavoring to a recipe. For instance, lemon juice added to sliced apples keeps them white. Guacamole retains its color for two to three days if lime juice is added. In this recipe the lime juice will slightly soften the finely sliced onion.

4 Cut the cucumber in half lengthwise, then use a teaspoon to scoop out the seeds. Slice the cucumber and add to the bowl. Remove the stem from the chile, slit it and scrape out the seeds with a small sharp knife. Chop the flesh finely and add to the bowl.

5 Add the sliced onion to the bowl, with any remaining lime juice, and mix well. Cover and let stand at room temperature for at least 1 hour before serving. If not serving immediately, put the salsa in the refrigerator; it will keep for 2–3 days.

SWEET POTATO

*VERY COLORFUL AND DELIGHTFULLY
TO HOT, SPICY MEXICAN DISHES.*

MAKES THE PERFECT ACCOMPANIMENT

SERVES FOUR AS AN ACCOMPANIMENT

INGREDIENTS

1½ pounds sweet potatoes
juice of 1 small orange
1 teaspoon crushed dried
  jalapeño chiles
4 small scallions
juice of 1 small lime (optional)
salt

and dice the
pan of water
otato and cook
st soft. Drain
in and put it
first turned
: potato dry
hen transfer

2 Mix the orange juice and crushed
dried chiles in a bowl. Chop the
scallions finely and add them to
the juice and chiles.

3 When the sweet potatoes are cool,
add the orange juice mixture and toss
carefully until all the pieces are coated.
Cover the bowl and chill for at least
1 hour, then taste and season with
salt. Stir in the lime juice, if you
prefer a fresher taste. The salsa will
keep for 2–3 days in a covered bowl in
the refrigerator.

COOK'S TIP

This fresh and tasty salsa is also very
good served with a simple grilled salmon
fillet or other fish dishes, and is a
delicious accompaniment to veal cutlets
or grilled chicken breasts.

NOPALES SALSA

Nopales are the tender, fleshy leaves or "paddles" of an edible cactus known variously as the cactus pear and the prickly pear cactus. This grows wild in Mexico, but is also cultivated. The most familiar type sold in Mexican markets has dark green ovals with tiny thorns. Fresh nopales are difficult to track down outside Mexico, but if you do locate a supply, look for paddles that are firm and smooth skinned.

SERVES FOUR AS AN ACCOMPANIMENT

INGREDIENTS

2 fresh red fresno chiles
9 ounces nopales (cactus paddles)
3 scallions
3 garlic cloves, peeled
½ red onion
3½ ounces fresh tomatillos
½ teaspoon salt
⅔ cup cider vinegar

1 Spear the chiles on a long-handled metal skewer and roast them over the flame of a gas burner until the skins blister and darken. Do not let the flesh burn. Alternatively, dry-fry them in a griddle until the skins are scorched. Place the roasted chiles in a strong plastic bag and tie the top to keep the steam in. Set aside for 20 minutes.

2 Remove the chiles from the bag and peel off the skins. Cut off the stems, then slit the chiles and scrape out the seeds. Chop the chiles roughly and set them aside.

COOK'S TIP
Fresh nopales are sometimes available at specialty fruit and vegetable stores. Like okra, they yield a sticky gum and are best boiled before being used. Fresh cactus will lose about half its weight during cooking. Look for canned nopales (sometimes sold as nopalitos) packed in water or vinegar.

6 Drain the mixture in a colander, rinse under cold running water to remove any remaining stickiness, then drain again. Discard the scallions and garlic.

3 Carefully remove the thorns from the nopales. Wearing gloves or holding each cactus paddle in turn with kitchen tongs, cut off the bumps that contain the thorns with a sharp knife.

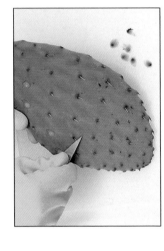

4 Cut off and discard the thick base from each cactus paddle. Rinse the paddles well and cut them into strips, then cut the strips into small pieces.

7 Chop the red onion and the tomatillos finely. Place in a bowl and add the cactus and chiles.

5 Bring a large saucepan of lightly salted water to a boil. Add the cactus paddle strips, scallions and garlic. Boil for 10–15 minutes, until the paddle strips are just tender.

8 Spoon the mixture into a large preserving jar, add the salt, pour in the vinegar and seal. Put the jar in the refrigerator for at least 1 day, turning the jar occasionally to ensure that the nopales are marinated. The salsa will keep in the refrigerator for up to 10 days.

MANGO SALSA

THIS HAS A FRESH, FRUITY TASTE AND IS PERFECT WITH FISH OR AS A CONTRAST TO RICH, CREAMY DISHES. THE BRIGHT COLORS MAKE IT AN ATTRACTIVE ADDITION TO ANY TABLE.

SERVES FOUR AS AN ACCOMPANIMENT

INGREDIENTS

2 fresh red fresno chiles
2 ripe mangoes
½ white onion
small bunch of cilantro
grated zest and juice of 1 lime

1 To peel the chiles, spear them on a long-handled metal skewer and roast them over the flame of a gas burner until the skins blister and darken. Do not let the flesh burn. Alternatively, dry-fry them in a griddle until the skins are scorched.

2 Place the roasted chiles in a strong plastic bag and tie the top to keep the steam in. Set aside for 20 minutes.

COOK'S TIP
Mangoes, in season, are readily available nowadays, but are usually sold unripe. Keep in a warm room for 24 hours or until they are just soft to the touch. Do not let ripen beyond this point.

3 Meanwhile, put one of the mangoes on a board and cut off a thick slice close to the flat side of the pit. Turn the mango around and repeat on the other side. Score the flesh on each thick slice with criss-cross lines at ½ inch intervals, taking care not to cut through the skin. Repeat with the second mango.

4 Fold the mango halves inside out so that the mango flesh stands proud of the skin, in neat dice. Carefully slice these off the skin and into a bowl. Cut off the flesh adhering to each pit, dice it and add it to the bowl.

5 Remove the roasted chiles from the bag and carefully peel off the skins. Cut off the stems, then slit the chiles and scrape out the seeds.

6 Chop the white onion and the cilantro finely and add them to the diced mango. Chop the chile flesh finely and add it to the mixture in the bowl, together with the lime zest and juice. Stir well to mix, cover and chill for at least 1 hour before serving. The salsa will keep for 2–3 days in the refrigerator.

ROASTED TOMATO AND CILANTRO SALSA

ROASTING THE TOMATOES GIVES A GREATER DEPTH TO THE FLAVOR OF THIS SALSA, WHICH ALSO BENEFITS FROM THE WARM, ROUNDED FLAVOR OF ROASTED CHILES.

SERVES SIX AS AN ACCOMPANIMENT

INGREDIENTS

1¼ pounds tomatoes
2 fresh serrano chiles
1 onion
juice of 1 lime
large bunch of cilantro
salt

1 Preheat the oven to 400°F. Cut the tomatoes into quarters and place them in a roasting pan. Add the chiles. Roast for 45 minutes–1 hour, until the tomatoes and chiles are charred and softened.

2 Place the roasted chiles in a strong plastic bag. Tie the top to keep the steam in and set aside for 20 minutes. Let the tomatoes cool slightly, then remove the skins and dice the flesh.

3 Chop the onion finely, then place in a bowl and add the lime juice and the chopped tomatoes.

4 Remove the chiles from the bag and peel off the skins. Cut off the stalks, then slit the chiles and scrape out the seeds with a sharp knife. Chop the chiles roughly and add them to the onion mixture. Mix well.

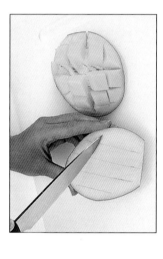

5 Chop the cilantro and add most to the salsa. Add salt, cover and chill for at least 1 hour before serving, sprinkled with the remaining cilantro. This salsa will keep in the refrigerator for 1 week.

RED RUB

This "rub" or dry paste is frequently used in the Yucatan for seasoning meat. The mixture is rubbed on the surface of the meat, which is then wrapped in banana leaves and cooked slowly in a pib, a heated stone-lined hole in the ground. Meat cooked this way is referred to as pibil-style. Try using the rub on pork chops or chicken pieces before baking or grilling.

MAKES ENOUGH FOR ONE ROAST
OR FOUR CHICKEN BREASTS

INGREDIENTS
2 teaspoons achiote (annatto) seeds
1 teaspoon black peppercorns
1 teaspoon allspice berries
1 teaspoon dried oregano
½ teaspoon ground cumin
1 teaspoon freshly squeezed lime juice
1 small Seville orange or ½ grapefruit

1 Put the achiote (annatto) seeds in a mortar and grind them with a pestle into a fine powder. Alternatively, use a food processor. Add the peppercorns, grind again, then repeat the process with the allspice berries. Mix in the oregano and ground cumin.

2 Add the lime juice to the spice mixture. Squeeze the orange or grapefruit and add the juice to the spice mixture a teaspoonful at a time until a thick paste is produced. Don't be tempted to substitute a sweet orange if Seville oranges are out of season; the spice mixture must be tart.

3 Let the paste stand for at least 30 minutes so the spices absorb the juice. The correct consistency for the paste is slightly dry and crumbly. When ready to use, rub the paste on the surface of the meat, then let marinate for at least 1 hour before cooking, preferably overnight. The rub will keep for up to 1 week in a covered bowl in the refrigerator, after which time some of the flavor will be lost.

COOK'S TIP

Achiote is the rusty red seed of the annatto, a tropical American tree. It is used in Mexico for flavoring and coloring cheeses, butter and smoked fish. It is also used in Indian cooking and can be purchased at ethnic food stores.

RED SALSA

Use this as a condiment with fish or meat dishes, or as a dipping sauce for baked potato wedges. It is often added to rice dishes.

MAKES ABOUT 1 CUP

INGREDIENTS
3 large tomatoes
1 tablespoon olive oil
3 ancho chiles
2 pasilla chiles
2 garlic cloves, peeled and left whole
2 scallions
2 teaspoons dark brown sugar
2.5ml/½ teaspoon paprika
juice of 1 lime
½ teaspoon dried oregano
salt

1 Preheat the oven to 400°F. Quarter the tomatoes and place in a roasting pan. Drizzle on the oil. Roast for about 40 minutes, until slightly charred, then remove the skin.

2 Soak the chiles in hot water for about 10 minutes. Drain, remove the stalks, slit and then scrape out the seeds. Chop finely. Dry-roast the garlic in a heavy pan, until golden.

3 Finely chop most of the scallions, retaining the top part of one for garnishing. Place the chopped onion in a bowl with the sugar, paprika, lime juice and oregano. Slice the remaining scallion diagonally, take out slices and set aside for the garnish.

4 Put the skinned tomatoes and chopped chiles in a food processor or blender and add the garlic cloves. Process until smooth.

5 Add the sugar, paprika, lime juice, scallions and oregano to the blender. Process for a few seconds, then taste and add salt as required. spoon into a saucepan and warm through before serving, or place in a bowl, cover and chill until needed. Garnish with the sliced scallions. The salsa will keep, covered, for up to 1 week in the refrigerator.

SO[UPS] AND S[NA]CKS

If you found the word "sopas" o[n] you might, quite rightly, translate it to mean "soups." However, your c[?] [q]uite what you were expecting. There are two classifications of [tho]se that conform to the accepted definition and consist o[f] fish cooked in a liquid, and those that come under [?] seca, or "dry soup." This may sound like a [?]ms, but there is actually a perfectly logical [?] seca starts out with plenty of liquid, but [?] rice, vermicelli or corn tortilla strips soon [?] [t]hat remains is a moist, thick, satisfying dish, [?] [?] course in the comida—the main meal— [?] may also be served solo.

Bocadit[os] [?]s," an apt description for a range of colorful little dishes th[e] [?]n throughout the day. Several of these may be served together, [?]s, to make an informal meal, or they may appear [?] a brunch or buffet table. Most bocaditos [?] [q]uickly and easily, so they make perfect [?] [?]ed lunches or picnic fare.

TLALPEÑO-STYLE SOUP

THIS SIMPLE CHICKEN SOUP ORIGINATES FROM TLALPAN, A SUBURB OF MEXICO CITY. THE SOUP IS MADE MORE SUBSTANTIAL BY THE ADDITION OF CHEESE AND CHICKPEAS.

SERVES SIX

INGREDIENTS

6¼ cups chicken stock
½ chipotle chile, seeded
2 skinless, boneless chicken breasts
1 medium avocado
4 scallions, finely sliced
14-ounce can chickpeas, drained
salt and ground black pepper
¾ cup grated Cheddar cheese,
to serve

1 Pour the stock into a large saucepan and add the dried chile. Bring to a boil, then add the whole chicken breasts, then lower the heat and simmer for about 10 minutes or until the chicken is cooked. Remove the chicken from the pan and let it cool a little.

2 Using two forks, shred the chicken into small pieces. Set it aside. Pour the stock and chile into a blender or food processor and process until smooth. Return the stock to the pan.

COOK'S TIP
When buying the avocado for this soup choose one that is slightly under-ripe, which makes it easier to handle when peeling and slicing.

3 Cut the avocado in half, remove the skin and pit, then slice the flesh into ¾-inch pieces. Add it to the stock, with the scallions and chickpeas. Return the shredded chicken to the pan, with salt and pepper to taste, and heat gently.

4 Spoon the soup into heated bowls. Sprinkle grated cheese on top of each portion and serve immediately.

CORN SOUP

QUICK AND EASY TO PREPARE, THIS COLORFUL SOUP HAS A SWEET FLAVOR. CHILDREN LOVE IT.

SERVES SIX

INGREDIENTS

2 red peppers
2 tablespoons vegetable oil
1 medium onion, finely chopped
3–4 cups corn niblets, thawed
   if frozen
3 cups chicken stock
⅔ cup light cream
salt and ground black pepper

1 Dry-fry the peppers in a griddle over medium heat, turning them frequently until the skins are blistered all over. Place them in a strong plastic bag and tie the top to keep the steam in. Set aside for 20 minutes, then remove the peppers from the bag and peel off the skin.

2 Cut the peppers in half and scoop out the seeds and cores. Set one aside. Cut the other into ½-inch dice.

3 Heat the oil in a large saucepan. Add the onion and sauté over low heat for about 10 minutes, until it is translucent and soft. Stir in the diced pepper and corn and cook for 5 minutes over medium heat.

4 Spoon the contents of the pan into a food processor, pour in the chicken stock and process until almost smooth. This processing can be done in batches if necessary.

5 Return the soup to the pan and reheat it. Stir in the cream, with salt and pepper to taste. Core, seed and cut the reserved pepper into thin strips and add half of these to the pan. Serve the soup in heated bowls, garnished with the remaining pepper strips.

COOK'S TIP
Look for roasted red peppers in jars. These come ready-skinned and are useful in all sorts of recipes. Used here, they make a quick soup even speedier.

TORTILLA SOUP

THERE ARE SEVERAL TORTILLA SOUPS. THIS ONE IS AN AGUADA—OR LIQUID—VERSION, AND IS INTENDED FOR SERVING AS AN APPETIZER OR LIGHT MEAL. IT IS VERY EASY AND QUICK TO PREPARE. YOU CAN ALSO MAKE IT IN ADVANCE AND FRY THE TORTILLA STRIPS AS IT REHEATS. THE CRISP TORTILLA PIECES ADD AN UNUSUAL TEXTURE.

SERVES FOUR

INGREDIENTS

4 corn tortillas, freshly made or a few
  days old
1 tablespoon vegetable oil, plus
  extra, for frying
1 small onion, finely chopped
2 garlic cloves, crushed
14-ounce can plum tomatoes, drained
4 cups chicken stock
small bunch of cilantro
salt and ground black pepper

1 Using a sharp knife, cut each tortilla into four or five strips, each measuring about ¾ inch wide.

2 Pour vegetable oil to a depth of ¾ inch into a heavy frying pan. Heat until a small piece of tortilla, added to the oil, floats on the top and bubbles at the edges.

3 Add a few tortilla strips to the hot oil and fry for a few minutes, until crisp and golden brown all over, turning them occasionally. Remove with a slotted spoon and drain on a double layer of paper towels. Cook the remaining tortilla strips in the same way.

4 Heat the 1 tablespoon vegetable oil in a large heavy saucepan. Add the chopped onion and garlic and cook over medium heat for 2–3 minutes, stirring constantly with a wooden spatula, until the onion is soft and translucent. Do not let the garlic turn brown or it will give the soup a bitter taste.

5 Chop the tomatoes using a large sharp knife and add them to the onion mixture in the pan. Pour in the chicken stock and stir well. Bring to a boil, then lower the heat and let simmer for about 10 minutes, until the liquid has reduced slightly.

6 Chop the cilantro. Add to the soup, reserving a little to use as a garnish. Season to taste.

7 Place a few of the crisp tortilla pieces in the bottom of four warmed soup bowls. Ladle the soup on top. Sprinkle each portion with the reserved chopped cilantro and serve.

COOK'S TIP

An easy way to chop the cilantro is to put the cilantro leaves in a mug and snip with a pair of scissors. Hold the scissors vertically in both hands and work the blades back and forth until the cilantro is finely chopped.

CHILLED COCONUT SOUP

Refreshing, cooling and not too filling, this soup is the perfect antidote to hot weather. For a formal meal, it would be an excellent choice for serving after an appetizer, to refresh the palate before the main course.

SERVES SIX

INGREDIENTS

5 cups milk
2⅔ cups unsweetened dry
    shredded coconut
1⅓ cups coconut milk
1⅔ cups chicken stock
scant 1 cup heavy cream
½ teaspoon salt
½ teaspoon ground white pepper
5ml/1 teaspoon sugar
small bunch of cilantro

COOK'S TIP

Avoid using sweetened coconut, which would spoil the flavor of this soup.

1 Pour the milk into a large saucepan. Bring it to a boil, stir in the coconut, lower the heat and let simmer for 30 minutes. Spoon the mixture into a food processor and process until smooth. This may take a while—up to 5 minutes—so pause frequently and scrape down the sides of the bowl.

2 Rinse the pan to remove any coconut that remains, pour in the processed mixture and add the coconut milk. Stir in the chicken stock (homemade, if possible, which gives a better flavor), cream, salt, pepper and sugar. Bring the mixture to a boil, stirring occasionally, then lower the heat and cook for 10 minutes.

3 Reserve a few cilantro leaves to garnish, then chop the rest finely and stir into the soup. Pour the soup into a large bowl, let it cool, then cover and put into the refrigerator until chilled. Just before serving, taste the soup and adjust the seasoning, as chilling will alter the taste. Serve in chilled bowls, garnished with the cilantro leaves.

AVOCADO SOUP

THIS DELICIOUS AND VERY PRETTY S[...]
FLAVOR. YOU MIGHT WANT TO ADD [...]

[...] DINNER PARTIES AND HAS A FRESH, DELICATE
[...]UICE JUST BEFORE SERVING FOR ADDED ZEST.

SERVES FOUR

INGREDIENTS

2 large ripe avocados
1¼ cups crème fraîche
4 cups well-flavored chicken stock
1 teaspoon salt
juice of ½ lime
small bunch of cilantro
½ teaspoon freshly ground
    black pepper

COOK'S TIP
Because this soup contains avocados, it
may discolor if left to stand, so make
it just before serving.

1 [...]emove the
pe[...]op the flesh
co[...]d processor
wit[...]crème
fra[...].

2 [...]a saucepan.
Wh[...]simmering
poi[...]rème
fra[...]

3 Add the lime juice to the avocado
mixture, process briefly to mix, then
gradually stir the mixture into the hot
stock. Heat gently but do not let the
mixture approach the boiling point.

4 Chop the cilantro. Pour the soup into
individual heated bowls and sprinkle
each portion with cilantro and black
pepper. Serve immediately.

CHILES RELLENOS

STUFFED CHILES ARE POPULAR ALL OVER MEXICO. THE TYPE OF CHILE USED DIFFERS FROM REGION TO REGION, BUT LARGER CHILES ARE OBVIOUSLY EASIER TO STUFF THAN SMALLER ONES. POBLANOS AND ANAHEIMS ARE QUITE MILD, BUT YOU CAN USE HOTTER CHILES IF YOU PREFER.

MAKES SIX

INGREDIENTS

6 fresh poblano or Anaheim chiles
2 potatoes, total weight about
    14 ounces
scant 1 cup cream cheese
1¾ cups grated aged
    Cheddar cheese
1 teaspoon salt
½ teaspoon ground black pepper
2 eggs, separated
1 cup all-purpose flour
½ teaspoon white pepper
oil, for frying
chile flakes to garnish, optional

1 Make a neat slit down one side of each chile. Place them in a dry frying pan over medium heat, turning them frequently until the skins blister.

2 Place the chiles in a strong plastic bag and tie the top to keep the steam in. Set aside for 20 minutes, then carefully peel off the skins and remove the seeds through the slits, keeping the chiles whole. Dry the chiles with paper towels and set them aside.

COOK'S TIP

Take care when making the filling; mix gently, trying not to break up the potato pieces.

VARIATION

Whole ancho (dried poblano) chiles can be used instead of fresh chiles, but will need to be reconstituted in water before they can be seeded and stuffed.

3 Scrub or peel the potatoes and cut them into ½ inch dice. Bring a large saucepan of water to the boil, add the potatoes and let the water return to the boiling point. Lower the heat and simmer for 5 minutes or until the potatoes are just tender. Do not overcook. Drain them thoroughly.

4 Put the cream cheese in a bowl and stir in the grated cheese, with ½ teaspoon of the salt and the black pepper. Add the potato and mix gently.

5 Spoon some of the potato filling into each chile. Put them on a plate, cover with plastic wrap and chill for 1 hour so that the filling becomes firm.

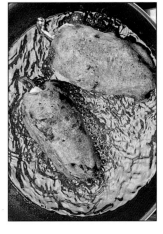

6 Put the egg whites in a clean, greasefree bowl and whisk them to firm peaks. In a separate bowl, beat the yolks until pale, then fold in the whites. Scrape the mixture onto a large, shallow dish. Spread out the flour in another shallow dish and season it with the remaining salt and the white pepper.

7 Heat the oil for deep frying to 375°F. Coat a few chiles first in flour and then in egg before adding carefully to the hot oil.

8 Fry the chiles in batches until golden and crisp. Drain on paper towels and serve hot, garnished with a sprinkle of chile flakes for extra heat, if desired.

EMPANADAS WITH ROPAS VIEJAS

THE FILLING FOR THESE EMPANADAS IS TRADITIONALLY MADE WITH MEAT THAT IS COOKED UNTIL IT IS SO TENDER THAT IT CAN BE TORN APART WITH FORKS. IT RESEMBLES TATTERED CLOTH, WHICH IS HOW IT CAME TO BE KNOWN AS ROPA VIEJA, WHICH MEANS "OLD CLOTHES."

SERVES SIX (TWELVE EMPANADAS)

INGREDIENTS

1 cup *masa harina*
2 tablespoons all-purpose flour
½ teaspoon salt
½–⅔ cup warm water
1 tablespoon oil, plus extra,
   for frying
9 ounces lean ground pork
1 garlic clove, crushed
3 tomatoes
2 ancho chiles
½ small onion
½ teaspoon ground cumin
½ teaspoon salt

1 Mix the *masa harina*, flour and salt in a bowl. Gradually add enough of the warm water to make a smooth, but not sticky, dough. Knead briefly, then shape into a ball, wrap in plastic wrap and set aside.

2 Heat 1 tablespoon oil in a saucepan. Add the pork and cook, stirring frequently, until it has browned evenly. Stir in the garlic and cook for 2 more minutes. Remove from heat and set the pan aside.

3 Cut a cross in the bottom of each tomato, place them in a bowl and pour over boiling water. After 3 minutes plunge the tomatoes into a bowl of cold water. Drain. The skins will peel back easily from the crosses. Remove the skins completely. Chop the tomato flesh and put in a bowl.

4 Slit the ancho chiles and scrape out the seeds. Chop the chiles finely and add them to the tomatoes. Chop the onion finely and add it to the tomato mixture, with the ground cumin.

5 Stir the tomato mixture into the pan containing the pork and cook over medium heat for 10 minutes, stirring occasionally. Season with salt to taste.

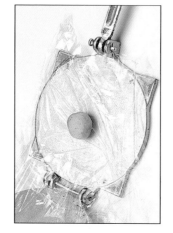

6 To make the tortillas, divide the empanada dough into 12 pieces and roll each piece into a ball. Open a tortilla press and line both sides with plastic (this can be cut from a new plastic sandwich bag). Put a ball of dough on the press and bring the top down to flatten it into a 3-inch round. Use the remaining dough balls to make more tortillas in the same way.

COOK'S TIP

If the empanada dough proves difficult to handle, a little oil or melted lard can be kneaded into the dough to help make it more pliable.

7 Spoon a little of the meat mixture on one half of each tortilla, working quickly to keep the dough from drying out. Dampen the edges of the dough with a little water and fold, turnover-style, to make the empanadas.

8 Seal the edges on the empanadas by pinching them between the index finger and thumb of the left hand and the index finger of the right hand.

9 Heat a little oil in a large frying pan. When it is hot, fry the empanadas in batches until crisp and golden on both sides, turning at least once. Serve hot or cold.

PANUCHOS

These stuffed tortillas are a bit fiddly to make, but well worth the effort. This dish is particularly popular in the Yucatán.

SERVES SIX (TWELVE *PANUCHOS*)

INGREDIENTS

1 cup *masa harina*
pinch of salt
½ cup warm water
2 skinless, boneless chicken breasts
1 teaspoon dried oregano
about 1 cup *Frijoles de Olla*, blended to a smooth purée
2 hard-boiled eggs, sliced
oil, for shallow-frying
salt and ground black pepper
Onion Relish, to serve

1 Mix the *masa harina* and salt in a large bowl. Add the warm water, a little at a time, to make a dough that can be worked into a ball. Knead this on a lightly floured surface for 3–4 minutes, until smooth, then wrap the dough in plastic wrap and let rest for 1 hour.

2 Put the chicken in a saucepan, add the dried oregano and pour in water to cover. Bring to a boil, then lower the heat and simmer for 10 minutes or until the chicken is cooked. Remove the chicken from the pan, discard the water and let the chicken cool a little. Using two forks, shred the chicken into small pieces. Set it aside.

3 Divide the dough into 12 small pieces and roll into balls. Open a tortilla press and line both sides with plastic (this can be cut from a new plastic sandwich bag). Put a dough ball on the press and flatten it into a 2½-inch round. Use the remaining dough balls to make more tortillas in the same way.

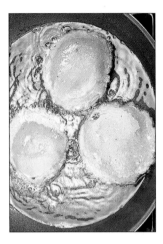

4 Cook each tortilla in a hot frying pan for 15–20 seconds on each side. After another 15 seconds on one side, remove and wrap in a clean dish towel.

5 Cut a slit in each tortilla, about ½ inch deep around the rim. Put a spoonful of the bean purée and a slice of hard-boiled egg in each slit.

6 Heat the oil for shallow frying in a large frying pan. Fry the tortilla pockets until they are crisp and golden brown on all sides, turning at least once during cooking. Drain them on paper towels and place on six individual serving plates. Top with a little of the shredded chicken and some onion relish. Season to taste and serve immediately.

SOPES WITH PICA...

THESE ARE SMALL, THICK TORTILLA... ...... HARINA WITH CRIMPED EDGES, WHICH ARE
FILLED LIKE TARTS. THEY ARE AN A... ...HEY REMAIN "DOUGHY" WHEN COOKED, BUT
THEY CAN BECOME QUITE ADDICTIV... ... CADILLO—IS VERY POPULAR IN MEXICO
AND IS USED IN MANY DIFFERENT R...

SERVES SIX

INGREDIENTS

scant 2 cups *masa harina*
½ teaspoon salt
¼ cup chilled lard
1¼ cups warm water
1 tablespoon vegetable oil
9 ounces lean ground beef
2 garlic cloves, crushed
1 red pepper, seeded and chopped
¼ cup dry sherry
1 tablespoon tomato paste
½ teaspoon ground cumin
1 teaspoon ground cinnamon
¼ teaspoon ground cloves
½ teaspoon ground black pepper
3 tablespoon raisins
¼ cup slivered almonds
fresh parsley sprigs, to garnish

2 Heat the oil in a large saucepan. Add the ground beef and cook over high heat, stirring until it has browned. Stir in the garlic and continue cooking for 2–3 minutes, stirring occasionally.

3 Stir in the red pepper, sherry, tomato purée and spices. Cook for 5 more minutes, then add the raisins and the slivered almonds. Lower the heat and simmer for 10 minutes. The meat should be cooked through and the mixture moist, but not wet. Keep hot.

4 Divide the dough into six balls. Open a tortilla press and line both sides with plastic (this can be cut from a new plastic sandwich bag). Put a ball on the press and bring the top down to flatten it into a 4-inch round, thicker than the conventional tortilla. Use the remaining dough balls to make five more rounds.

5 Heat a griddle or frying pan until hot. Add one of the rounds and fry until the underside is beginning to brown and blister. Turn the round over and cook the other side briefly, until the color is just beginning to change. Slide onto a plate and crimp the rim to form a raised edge. Fill with the spicy beef and keep hot while cooking and filling the remaining tartlets. Garnish with parsley.

COOK'S TIP
Take care that the dough for the *sopes* does not become dry. Wrap it in plastic wrap while it is set aside.

QUESADILLAS

These cheese-filled tortillas are the Mexican equivalent of grilled cheese sandwiches. Serve them as soon as they are cooked, or they will become chewy. If you are making them for a crowd, fill and fold the tortillas ahead of time, but only cook them to order.

<u>SERVES FOUR</u>

INGREDIENTS

7 ounces mozzarella, Monterey Jack
  or mild Cheddar cheese
1 fresh fresno chile (optional)
8 flour tortillas, about
  6-inches across
Onion Relish or Classic Tomato Salsa,
  to serve

VARIATIONS
Try spreading a thin layer of your favorite Mexican salsa on the tortilla before adding the cheese, or adding a few pieces of cooked chicken or shrimp before folding the tortilla in half.

1 If using mozzarella cheese, it must be drained thoroughly and then patted dry and sliced into thin strips. Monterey Jack and Cheddar cheese should both be coarsely grated, as finely grated cheese will melt and ooze out when cooking. Set the cheese aside in a bowl.

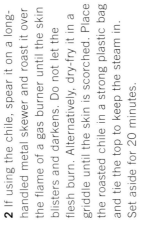

2 If using the chile, spear it on a long-handled metal skewer and roast it over the flame of a gas burner until the skin blisters and darkens. Do not let the flesh burn. Alternatively, dry-fry it in a griddle until the skin is scorched. Place the roasted chile in a strong plastic bag and tie the top to keep the steam in. Set aside for 20 minutes.

3 Remove the chile from the bag and peel off the skin. Cut off the stem, then slit the chile and scrape out the seeds. Cut the flesh into eight thin strips.

4 Warm a large frying pan or griddle. Place one tortilla on the pan or griddle at a time, sprinkle about an eighth of the cheese on one half and add a strip of chile, if using. Fold the tortilla over the cheese and press the edges together gently to seal. Cook the filled tortilla for 1 minute, then turn over and cook the other side for 1 minute.

5 Remove the filled tortilla from the pan or griddle, cut it into three triangles or four strips and serve immediately, with the onion relish or tomato salsa.

MEXICAN RICE

VERSIONS OF THIS DISH—A RELATI... —ARE POPULAR ALL OVER SOUTH AMERICA. CLASSIFIED AS A SOPA SECA OR DR... CIOUS MEDLEY OF RICE, TOMATOES AND AROMATIC FLAVORINGS. THE STOCK ... IS COOKED IS LARGELY ABSORBED BY THE TIME THE DISH IS READY TO BE SERV...

SERVES SIX

INGREDIENTS

1 cup long-grain rice
7-ounce can chopped tomatoes in
    tomato juice
½ onion, roughly chopped
2 garlic cloves, roughly chopped
2 tablespoons vegetable oil
scant 2 cups chicken stock
½ teaspoon salt
3 fresh fresno chiles or other fresh
    green chiles, trimmed
1 cup frozen peas (optional)
    ground black pepper

1 Put the rice in a large heatproof bowl and pour in boiling water to cover. Stir once, then let stand for 10 minutes. Transfer to a strainer over the sink, rinse under cold water, then drain again. Set aside to dry slightly.

2 M... ...es and juice ... ...blender, add ... process until ...

3 Hea... pan, add th... dium heat u... golden brown ... re that the ric... of the ...ttom

4 Add the tomato mixture and stir over medium heat until all the liquid has been absorbed. Stir in the stock, salt, whole chiles and peas, if using. Continue to cook the mixture, stirring occasionally, until all the liquid has been absorbed and the rice is just tender.

5 Remove the pan from the heat, cover it with a tight-fitting lid and let it stand in a warm place for 5–10 minutes. Remove the chiles, fluff up the rice lightly and serve, sprinkled with black pepper. The chiles may be used as a garnish, if desired.

COOK'S TIP
Do not stir the rice too often after adding the stock or the grains will break down and the mixture will become starchy.

CHICKEN FLAUTAS

Crisp fried tortillas with a chicken and cheese filling make a delicious light meal, especially when served with a spicy tomato salsa. The secret of success is to make sure that the oil is sufficiently hot to prevent the flutes from absorbing too much of it.

MAKES TWELVE

INGREDIENTS

2 skinless, boneless chicken breasts
1 onion
2 garlic cloves
1 tablespoon vegetable oil
3½ ounces feta cheese, crumbled
12 corn tortillas, freshly made or a few days old
oil, for frying
salt and ground black pepper

For the salsa
3 tomatoes, peeled, seeded and chopped
juice of ½ lime
small bunch of cilantro, chopped
½ small onion, finely chopped
3 fresh fresno chiles or similar fresh green chiles, seeded and chopped

1 Start by making the salsa. Mix the tomatoes, lime juice, coriander, onion and chiles in a bowl. Season with salt to taste and set aside.

2 Put the chicken breasts in a large saucepan, add water to cover and bring to a boil. Lower the heat and simmer for 15–20 minutes or until the chicken is cooked. Remove the chicken from the pan and let it cool a little. Using two forks, shred the chicken into small pieces. Set it aside.

3 Chop the onion finely and crush the garlic. Heat the oil in a frying pan, add the onion and garlic and sauté over low heat for about 5 minutes or until the onion has softened but not colored. Add the shredded chicken, with salt and pepper to taste. Mix well, remove from heat and stir in the feta.

4 Before they can be rolled, soften the tortillas by steaming three or four at a time on a plate over boiling water for a few moments until they are pliable. Alternatively, wrap them in microwave-safe film and then heat them in a microwave oven on full power for about 30 seconds.

5 Place a spoonful of the chicken filling on one of the tortillas. Roll the tortilla tightly around the filling to make a neat cylinder. Secure with a toothpick. Immediately cover the roll with plastic wrap to prevent the tortilla from drying out and splitting. Fill and roll the remaining tortillas in the same way.

6 Pour oil into a frying pan to a depth of 1 inch. Heat it until a small cube of bread, added to the oil, rises to the surface and bubbles at the edges before turning golden. Remove the cocktail sticks, then add the flutes to the pan, a few at a time.

7 Fry the flutes for 2–3 minutes, until golden, turning frequently. Drain on paper towels and serve immediately, with the salsa.

COOK'S TIP
You might find it easier to keep the cocktail sticks in place until after the flutes have been fried, in which case remove them before serving.

EGGS WITH CHORIZO

In Mexico, there are two types of chorizo sausage. The first is freshly made and sold loose; the second is packed in sausage skins and air-dried, like Spanish chorizo. This is a recipe for the former. Freshly made chorizo can be used in a number of savory dishes, but is particularly good with scrambled eggs, as here.

<u>SERVES FOUR</u>

INGREDIENTS

2 tablespoons lard
1¼ pounds ground pork
3 garlic cloves, crushed
2 teaspoons dried oregano
1 teaspoon ground cinnamon
½ teaspoon ground cloves
½ teaspoon ground black pepper
2 tablespoons dry sherry
1 teaspoon caster sugar
1 teaspoon salt
6 eggs
2 tomatoes, peeled, seeded and finely diced
½ small onion, finely chopped
¼ cup milk or light cream
fresh oregano sprigs, to garnish
warm corn or flour tortillas, to serve

1 Melt the lard in a large frying pan over medium heat. Add the pork mince and cook until browned, stirring frequently. Stir in the garlic, dried oregano, cinnamon, cloves and black pepper. Cook for 3–4 more minutes.

2 Add the sherry, sugar and salt to the pork, stir well and cook for 3–4 minutes, until the flavors are blended. Remove from heat.

3 Put the eggs in a bowl. Beat lightly to mix, then stir in the finely diced tomatoes and chopped onion.

4 Return the chorizo mixture to the heat. Heat it through and pour in the egg mixture. Cook, stirring constantly, until the egg is almost firm.

5 Stir in the milk or cream and check the seasoning. Garnish with fresh oregano and serve with warm corn or flour tortillas.

CHILES IN CHEESE SAUCE

This makes an excellent appetizer, light lunch or dip to serve with drinks. The chiles and tequila give it quite a kick.

<u>SERVES FOUR TO SIX</u>

INGREDIENTS

4 fresh fresno chiles or other fresh green chiles
1 tablespoon vegetable oil
½ red onion, finely chopped
5 cups grated Monterey Jack cheese
2 tablespoons crème fraîche
⅔ cup heavy cream
2 firm tomatoes, peeled
1 tablespoon reposada tequila
Tortilla Chips, to serve

COOK'S TIP

Cross-cut the bottom of a tomato and cover with boiling water. Plunge into cold water and the skin will peel off easily.

1 Place the chiles in a dry frying pan over medium heat, turning them frequently until the skin blisters and darkens. Place the chiles in a strong plastic bag and tie the top to keep the steam in. Set aside for 20 minutes, then carefully peel off the skins. Slit the chiles and scrape out the seeds, then cut the flesh into thin strips. Cut these in half lengthwise.

2 Heat the oil in a frying pan and sauté the onion over medium heat for 5 minutes, until it is beginning to soften. Add the cheese, crème fraîche and cream. Stir over low heat until the cheese melts and the mixture becomes a rich, creamy sauce. Stir in the thick chile strips.

3 Cut the tomatoes in half and scrape out the seeds. Cut the flesh into ½-inch pieces and stir these into the sauce.

4 Just before serving, stir in the tequila. Pour the sauce into a serving dish and serve warm, with the tortilla chips.

MOLETTES

THIS IS THE MEXICAN VERSION OF BEANS ON TOAST. SOLD BY STREET TRADERS AROUND MID-MORNING, THEY MAKE THE PERFECT SNACK FOR THOSE WHO HAVE MISSED BREAKFAST.

<u>SERVES FOUR</u>

INGREDIENTS
4 crusty rolls
¼ cup butter, softened
1⅓ cups Refried Beans
1¼ cups grated Cheddar cheese
green salad leaves, to garnish
½ cup Classic Tomato Salsa,
   to serve

1 Cut the rolls in half, then take a sliver off the bottom so that they lie flat. Remove a little of the insides. Spread them lightly with enough butter to crisp.

2 Arrange them on a baking sheet and broil for about 5 minutes or until they are crisp and golden. Meanwhile, heat the refried beans over low heat in a small saucepan.

3 Scoop the beans into the rolls, then sprinkle the grated cheese on top. Pop back under the broiler until the cheese melts. Serve with the tomato salsa and garnish with salad leaves.

EGGS MOTULENOS

A TASTY AND FILLING BREAKFAST OR MIDDAY SNACK, BLACK BEANS, WHICH ARE ALSO KNOWN AS TURTLE BEANS, ARE TOPPED WITH EGGS AND CHILI SAUCE AND SURROUNDED BY PEAS AND HAM.

<u>SERVES FOUR</u>

INGREDIENTS
generous 1 cup black beans, soaked
   overnight in water
1 small onion, finely chopped
2 garlic cloves
small bunch of cilantro, chopped
1 cup frozen peas
4 corn tortillas
2 tablespoons oil
4 eggs
5 ounces cooked ham, diced
4 tablespoons hot chili sauce
3 ounces feta cheese, crumbled
salt and ground black pepper
Classic Tomato Salsa, to serve

1 Drain the beans, rinse them under cold water and drain again. Put them in a saucepan, add the onion and garlic and water to cover. Bring to a boil, then simmer for 40 minutes. Stir in the cilantro, with salt and pepper to taste, and keep the beans hot.

2 Cook the peas in a small saucepan of boiling water until they are just tender. Drain and set aside. Wrap the tortillas in aluminium foil and place them on a plate. Stand the plate over a pan of boiling water and steam them for about 5 minutes. Alternatively, wrap them in microwave plastic wrap and heat them in a microwave on full power for about 30 seconds.

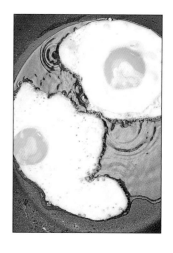

3 Heat the oil in a frying pan and fry the eggs until the whites are set. Lift them onto a plate and keep them warm while you quickly heat the ham and peas in the oil remaining in the pan.

4 Place the tortillas on warmed plates and top each one with some beans. Place an egg on each tortilla, spoon on 1 tablespoon hot chili sauce, then surround each egg with some peas and ham. Sprinkle feta on the peas and serve immediately, with salsa on the side.

EGGS RANCHEROS

THERE ARE MANY VARIATIONS ON THIS POPULAR DISH, WHICH IS GREAT FOR BREAKFAST OR BRUNCH. THE COMBINATION OF CREAMY EGGS WITH ONION, CHILE AND TOMATOES WORKS WONDERFULLY WELL.

SERVES FOUR FOR BREAKFAST

INGREDIENTS

2 corn tortillas, several days old
oil, for frying
2 fresh green jalapeño chiles
1 garlic clove
4 scallions
1 large tomato
8 eggs, beaten
⅔ cup light cream
small bunch of cilantro,
    finely chopped
salt and ground black pepper

1 Cut the tortillas into long strips. Pour oil into a frying pan to a depth of ½ inch. Heat the oil until it is very hot, watching it closely.

2 Fry the tortilla strips in batches for a minute or two until they are crisp and golden, turning them occasionally, then drain on paper towels.

COOK'S TIP

When cooking the tortilla strips it is important that the oil is the correct temperature. To test if the oil is ready to use, carefully add a strip of tortilla. If the strip floats and the oil immediately bubbles around its edges, the oil is ready.

3 Spear the chiles on a long-handled metal skewer and roast them over the flame of a gas burner until the skins blister and darken. Do not let the flesh burn. Alternatively, dry-fry them in a griddle until the skins are scorched. Place them in a strong plastic bag and tie the top to keep the steam in. Set aside for 20 minutes.

4 Meanwhile, crush the garlic and chop the scallions finely. Cut a cross in the bottom of the tomato. Place it in a heatproof bowl and pour on boiling water to cover. After 3 minutes, lift the tomato out using a slotted spoon and plunge it into a bowl of cold water. Let sit for a few minutes to cool.

5 Drain the tomato, remove the skin and cut it into four pieces. Using a teaspoon scoop out the seeds and the core, then dice the flesh finely.

6 Remove the chiles from the bag and peel off the skins. Cut off the stems, then slit the chiles and scrape out the seeds. Chop the flesh finely. Put the eggs in a bowl, season with salt and pepper and beat lightly.

7 Heat 1 tablespoon oil in a large frying pan. Add the garlic and scallions and sauté gently for 2–3 minutes, until soft. Stir in the diced tomato and cook for 3–4 more minutes, then stir in the chiles and cook for 1 minute.

8 Pour the eggs into the pan and stir until they start to set. When only a small amount of uncooked egg remains visible, stir in the cream so that the cooking process is slowed down and the mixture cooks into a creamy mixture rather than a solid mass.

9 Stir the chopped cilantro into the scrambled eggs. Arrange the tortilla strips on four serving plates and spoon on the eggs. Serve immediately.

TORTILLA CHIPS

THESE ARE KNOWN AS TOTOPOS IN MEXICO, AND THE TERM REFERS TO BOTH THE FRIED TORTILLA STRIPS USED TO GARNISH SOUPS AND THE TRIANGLES OF CORN TORTILLA USED FOR SCOOPING SALSA OR DIPS. USE TORTILLAS THAT ARE A FEW DAYS OLD; FRESH ONES WILL NOT CRISP UP AS WELL.

SERVES FOUR

INGREDIENTS
4–8 corn tortillas
oil, for frying
salt

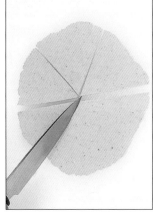

1 Cut each tortilla into six triangular wedges. Pour oil into a large frying pan to a depth of ½ inch, place the pan over medium heat and heat until very hot (see Cook's Tip).

2 Fry the tortilla wedges in the hot oil in small batches until they turn golden and are crisp. This will only take a few moments. Remove with a slotted spoon and drain on paper towels. Sprinkle with salt.

3 *Totopos* should be served warm. They can be cooled completely and stored in an airtight container for a few days, but will need to be reheated in a microwave or a warm oven before being served.

COOK'S TIP
The oil needs to be very hot for cooking the tortillas—test it by carefully adding one of the wedges. It should float and begin to bubble in the oil immediately.

VARIATION
When fried, flour tortillas do not crisp up as well as corn tortillas, but they make a delicious sweet treat when sprinkled with ground cinnamon and sugar. Serve them hot with cream.

PEPITAS

THESE LITTLE SNACKS ARE ABSOLUTELY IRRESISTIBLE, ESPECIALLY IF YOU INCLUDE CHIPOTLE CHILES. THEIR SMOKY FLAVOR IS THE PERFECT FOIL FOR THE NUTTY TASTE OF THE PUMPKIN SEEDS AND THE SWEETNESS CONTRIBUTED BY THE SUGAR. SERVE THEM WITH PRE-DINNER DRINKS.

SERVES FOUR

INGREDIENTS
1 cup pumpkin seeds
4 garlic cloves, crushed
¼ teaspoon salt
2 teaspoons crushed dried chiles
1 teaspoon sugar
a wedge of lime

COOK'S TIP
It is important to keep the pumpkin seeds moving as they cook. Watch them carefully and do not let them burn, or they will taste bitter.

1 Heat a small heavy frying pan, add the pumpkin seeds and dry-fry for a few minutes, stirring constantly as they swell.

2 When all the seeds have swollen, add the garlic and cook for a few more minutes, stirring constantly. Add the salt and the crushed chiles and stir to mix. Turn off the heat, but keep the pan on the stove. Sprinkle sugar on the seeds and shake the pan to ensure that they are all coated.

3 Transfer the *pepitas* to a bowl and serve with the wedge of lime for squeezing on the seeds. If the lime is omitted, the seeds can be cooled and stored in an airtight container for reheating later, but they are best served fresh.

SPICED PLANTAIN CHIPS

PLANTAINS ARE MORE STARCHY THAN THE BANANAS TO WHICH THEY ARE RELATED, AND MUST BE COOKED BEFORE BEING EATEN. IN LATIN AMERICA THE FRUIT IS USED MUCH AS A POTATO WOULD BE. THIS SNACK HAS A LOVELY SWEET TASTE, WHICH IS BALANCED BY THE HEAT FROM THE CHILI POWDER AND SAUCE. COOK THE CHIPS JUST BEFORE YOU PLAN TO SERVE THEM.

SERVES FOUR AS AN APPETIZER OR SNACK

INGREDIENTS

2 large plantains
oil, for shallow-frying
½ teaspoon chili powder
1 teaspoon ground cinnamon
hot chili sauce, to serve

COOK'S TIP

Plantain skins are very dark, almost black, when the fruit is ready to eat. If they are green when you buy them, let them ripen at room temperature for a few days before use.

1 Peel the plantains. Cut off and throw away the ends, then slice the fruit into rounds, cutting slightly on the diagonal to give larger, flatter slices.

2 Pour the oil for frying into a small frying pan, to a depth of about ½ inch. Heat the oil until it is very hot, watching it closely. Test by carefully adding a slice of plantain; it should float and the oil should immediately bubble up around it.

3 Fry the plantain slices in small batches or the temperature of the oil will drop. When they are golden brown, remove from the oil with a slotted spoon and drain on paper towels.

4 Mix the chili powder with the cinnamon. Put the plantain chips on a serving plate, sprinkle them with the chili and cinnamon mixture and serve immediately, with a small bowl of hot chili sauce for dipping.

POPCORN WITH L[IME AND C]HILI

IF THE ONLY POPCORN YOU'VE HAD
SPECIALTY. THE LIME JUICE AND CH[ILI]
A HEALTHY CHOICE TO SERVE WITH

[PO]RTION AT THE MOVIES, TRY THIS MEXICAN
[INS]PIRED ADDITIONS, AND THE SNACK IS QUITE

MAKES ONE LARGE BOWL

INGREDIENTS

2 tablespoons vegetable oil
1¼ cups corn kernels
    for popcorn
2 teaspoons chili powder
juice of 2 limes

1 Heat the oil in a large, heavy frying pan until it is very hot. Add the popcorn and immediately cover the pan with a lid and reduce the heat.

2 After a few minutes the corn should start to pop. Resist the temptation to lift the lid to check. Shake the pan occasionally so that all corn will be cooked and browned.

3 [...]g corn has [...]sto[...] pan from [...]the[...] off[...]. Take [...] lift out and [...] dis[...] t have not [...] pop[...] will have [...] fall[...] in and is [...] cor[...]

4 Add the chili powder. Shake the pan again and again to make sure that all of the corn is covered with a colorful dusting of chili.

5 Transfer the popcorn to a large bowl and keep warm. Add a squeeze of lime juice immediately before serving.

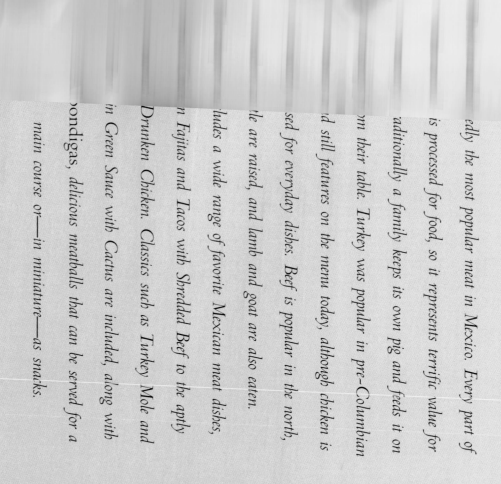

DISHES

edly the most popular meat in Mexico. Every part of
is processed for food, so it represents terrific value for
aditionally a family keeps its own pig and feeds it on
om their table. Turkey was popular in pre-Columbian
d still features on the menu today, although chicken is
sed for everyday dishes. Beef is popular in the north,
le are raised, and lamb and goat are also eaten.
ludes a wide range of favorite Mexican meat dishes,
n Fajitas and Tacos with Shredded Beef to the aptly
Drunken Chicken. Classics such as Turkey Mole and
in Green Sauce with Cactus are included, along with
ondigas, delicious meatballs that can be served for a
main course or—in miniature—as snacks.

BURRITOS WITH CHICKEN AND RICE

IN MEXICO, BURRITOS ARE A POPULAR STREET FOOD, EATEN ON THE RUN. THE SECRET OF A SUCCESSFUL BURRITO IS TO HAVE ALL THE FILLING NEATLY PACKAGED INSIDE THE TORTILLA FOR EASY EATING, SO THESE SNACKS ARE SELDOM SERVED WITH A POUR-ON SAUCE.

SERVES FOUR

INGREDIENTS

½ cup long grain rice
1 tablespoon vegetable oil
1 onion, chopped
½ teaspoon ground cloves
1 teaspoon dried, or fresh oregano
7-ounce can chopped tomatoes in tomato juice
2 skinless, boneless chicken breasts
1¼ cups grated Monterey Jack or mild Cheddar cheese
4 tablespoons sour cream (optional)
8 x 8–10-inch fresh flour tortillas
salt
fresh oregano, to garnish (optional)

1 Bring a saucepan of lightly salted water to a boil. Add the rice and cook for 8 minutes. Drain, rinse and then drain again.

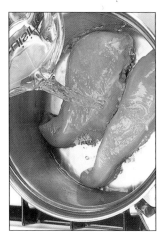

2 Heat the oil in a large saucepan. Add the onion, with the ground cloves and oregano, and fry for 2–3 minutes. Stir in the rice and tomatoes and cook over low heat until all the tomato juice has been absorbed. Set the pan aside.

3 Put the chicken breasts in a large saucepan, pour in enough water to cover and bring to a boil. Lower the heat and simmer for about 10 minutes or until the chicken is cooked through. Lift the chicken out of the pan, put on a plate and cool slightly.

4 Preheat the oven to 325°F. Shred the chicken by pulling the flesh apart with two forks, then add the chicken to the rice mixture, with the grated cheese. Stir in the sour cream, if using.

5 Wrap the tortillas in aluminum foil and place them on a plate. Stand the plate over boiling water for about 5 minutes. Alternatively, wrap in microwave-safe plastic wrap and heat in a microwave on full power for 1 minute.

6 Spoon one-eighth of the filling into the center of a tortilla and fold in both sides. Fold the bottom up and the top down to form a parcel. Secure with a toothpick.

7 Put the filled burrito in a shallow dish or casserole, cover with foil and keep warm in the oven while you make seven more. Remove the toothpicks before serving, sprinkled with fresh oregano.

COOK'S TIP

If you use very fresh tortillas, you may be able to dispense with the toothpicks. Secure the tortilla parcels by damping the final fold with a little water. When you lay the burritos in the dish, place them with the folded surfaces down.

CHICKEN AND TOMATILLO CHIMICHANGAS

THESE FRIED BURRITOS ARE A COMMON SIGHT ON STREET STALLS AND IN CAFÉS ALONG THE MEXICAN BORDER WITH TEXAS, BUT ARE NOT SO WELL KNOWN FURTHER SOUTH.

SERVES FOUR

INGREDIENTS

2 skinless, boneless chicken breasts
1 chipotle chile, seeded
1 tablespoon vegetable oil
2 onions, finely chopped
4 garlic cloves, crushed
½ teaspoon ground cumin
½ teaspoon ground coriander
½ teaspoon ground cinnamon
½ teaspoon ground cloves
scant 2 cups drained canned
   tomatillos
2⅓ cups cooked pinto beans
8 x 8–10-inch fresh flour
   tortillas
oil, for frying
salt and ground black pepper

1 Put the chicken breasts in a large saucepan, pour in water to cover and add the chile. Bring to a boil, lower the heat and simmer for 10 minutes or until the chicken is cooked through and the chile has softened. Remove the chile and chop it finely. Lift the chicken breasts out of the pan and put them on a plate. Let cool slightly, then shred with two forks.

2 Heat the oil in a frying pan. Sauté the onions until translucent, then add the garlic and ground spices and cook for 3 more minutes. Add the tomatillos and pinto beans. Cook over medium heat for 5 minutes, stirring constantly to break up the tomatillos and some of the beans. Simmer gently for 5 more minutes. Add the chicken and seasoning.

3 Wrap the tortillas in aluminum foil and place them on a plate. Stand the plate over boiling water for about 5 minutes until they become pliable. Alternatively, wrap them in microwave-safe plastic wrap and heat them in a microwave on full power for 1 minute.

4 Spoon one-eighth of the bean filling into the center of a tortilla, fold in both sides, then fold the bottom of the tortilla up and the top down to form a neat parcel. Secure with a toothpick.

5 Heat the oil in a large frying pan and fry the chimichangas in batches until crisp, turning once. Remove them from the oil with a slotted spoon and drain on paper towels. Serve hot.

COOK'S TIP
The word "pinto" means speckled, which aptly describes these attractive dried beans. If you prepare them yourself, they will need to be soaked overnight in water, then cooked in unsalted boiling water for 1–1¼ hours, until tender.

DRUNKEN CHI[CKEN]

TEQUILA IS THIS CHICKEN'S MAG... FLAVOR. SERVE IT WITH GREEN O...

THE DISH HAS A DELICIOUS SWEET-AND-SOUR FLAVOR.

FLOUR TORTILLAS TO MOP UP THE SAUCE.

SERVES FOUR

INGREDIENTS

scant 1 cup raisins
½ cup sherry
1 cup all-purpose flour
½ teaspoon salt
½ teaspoon ground black pepper
3 tablespoons vegetable oil
8 skinless chicken thighs, bone-ir
1 onion, halved and thinly sliced
3 garlic cloves, crushed
2 tart apples, such as Granny Smith
1 cup slivered almonds
1 ripe plantain, peeled and slice
1½ cups well-flavored chicken st
1 cup tequila
fresh herbs, chopped, to garnish (optional)

in a bowl and pour in
side to plump up.
with the salt and
ad it out on a large, flat
off the lid and cook for 10 more minutes
e. Heat 2 tablespoons
ge frying pan. Dip each
turn in the seasoned
the hot oil until
g occasionally. Drain

2 Heat the remaining vegetable oil in a large, deep frying pan. Add the onion slices and crushed garlic and cook for 2–3 minutes. Meanwhile, peel, core and dice the apples.

3 Add the diced apple to the onion mixture with the almonds and plantain slices. Cook, stirring occasionally, for 3–4 minutes, then add the soaked raisins, with any remaining sherry. Add the chicken pieces to the pan.

the chicken mixture. Cover the pan with a lid and cook for 15 minutes, then take off the lid and cook for 10 more minutes or until the sauce has reduced by about half.

4 Pour the stock and tequila over the

5 Check that the chicken thighs are cooked by lifting one out of the pan and piercing it in the thickest part with a sharp knife or skewer. Any juices that come out should be clear. If necessary, cook the chicken for a little longer before serving, sprinkled with chopped fresh herbs, if desired.

CHICKEN FAJITAS

THE PERFECT DISH FOR CASUAL ENTERTAINING, FAJITAS ARE FLOUR TORTILLAS THAT ARE
BROUGHT TO THE TABLE FRESHLY COOKED. GUESTS ADD THEIR OWN FILLINGS BEFORE FOLDING
UP THE TORTILLAS.

SERVES SIX

INGREDIENTS

3 skinless, boneless chicken breasts
finely grated zest and juice of
  2 limes
2 tablespoons sugar
2 teaspoons dried oregano
½ teaspoon cayenne pepper
1 teaspoon ground cinnamon
2 onions
3 bell peppers (1 red, 1 yellow or
  orange and 1 green)
3 tablespoons vegetable oil
guacamole, salsa and sour cream,
  to serve
For the tortillas
2¼ cups all-purpose flour, sifted
¼ teaspoon baking powder
pinch of salt
¼ cup lard
¼ cup warm water

COOK'S TIP

Tortilla dough can be very difficult to roll
out thinly. If the dough is breaking up,
try placing each ball between two sheets
of clean plastic wrap (this can be cut
from a new sandwich bag). Roll out,
turning over, still inside the plastic, until
the tortilla is the right size.

1 Slice the chicken breasts into ¾-inch
wide strips and place these in a large
bowl. Add the lime zest and juice,
sugar, oregano, cayenne and cinnamon.
Mix thoroughly. Set aside to marinate for
at least 30 minutes.

2 Meanwhile, make the tortillas. Mix the
flour, baking powder and salt in a large
bowl. Rub in the lard, then add the
warm water, a little at a time, to make a
stiff dough. Knead this on a lightly
floured surface for 10–15 minutes, until
it is smooth and elastic.

3 Divide the dough into 12 small balls,
then roll each ball into a 6-inch round.
Cover the rounds with plastic wrap to
keep them from drying out while you
prepare the vegetables.

4 Cut the onions in half and slice them
thinly. Cut the peppers in half, remove
the cores and seeds, then slice the
flesh into ½ inch wide strips.

5 Heat a large frying pan or griddle and
cook each tortilla in turn for about
1 minute on each side or until the
surface colors and begins to blister.
Keep the cooked tortillas warm and
pliable by wrapping them in a clean,
dry dish towel.

6 Heat the oil in a large frying pan.
Stir-fry the marinated chicken for
5–6 minutes, then add the peppers and
onions and cook for 3–4 more minutes
more, until the chicken strips are
cooked through and the vegetables
are soft and tender, but still juicy.

7 Spoon the chicken mixture into a
serving bowl and take it to the table
with the cooked tortillas, guacamole,
salsa and sour cream. Keep the tortillas
wrapped and warm.

8 To serve, each guest takes a warm
tortilla, spreads it with a little salsa, adds
a spoonful of guacamole and piles some
of the chicken mixture in the center. The
final touch is to add a small dollop of
sour cream. The tortilla is then folded
over the filling and eaten.

CHICKEN WITH CHIPOTLE SAUCE

IT IS IMPORTANT TO USE CHIPOTLE CHILES IN THIS RECIPE, AS THEY IMPART A WONDERFULLY RICH AND SMOKY FLAVOR TO THE CHICKEN BREASTS. THE PURÉE CAN BE MADE AHEAD OF TIME, MAKING THIS A VERY EASY RECIPE FOR ENTERTAINING.

SERVES SIX

INGREDIENTS

6 chipotle chiles
scant 1 cup water
chicken stock (see method)
3 onions
6 boneless chicken breasts
3 tablespoons vegetable oil
salt and ground black pepper
fresh oregano to garnish

3 Peel the onions. Using a sharp knife, cut them in half, then slice them thinly. Separate the slices.

4 Remove the skin from the chicken breasts and trim off any stray pieces of fat or membrane.

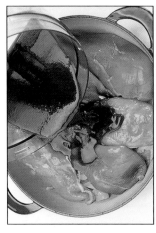

7 Arrange the chicken breasts on top of the onion slices. Sprinkle with a little salt and several grindings of black pepper.

1 Put the dried chiles in a bowl and pour in hot water to cover. Let stand for about 30 minutes, until very soft. Drain, reserving the soaking water in a measuring cup. Cut off the stem from each chile, then slit them lengthwise and scrape out the seeds with a small sharp knife.

2 Preheat the oven to 350°F. Chop the flesh of the chiles roughly and put it in a food processor or blender. Add enough chicken stock to the soaking water to make 1⅔ cups. Pour it into the processor or blender and process at maximum power until smooth.

5 Heat the oil in a large frying pan, add the onions and cook over low to medium heat for about 5 minutes or until they have softened but not colored, stirring occasionally.

6 Using a slotted spoon, transfer the onion slices to a casserole that is large enough to hold all the chicken breasts in a single layer. Sprinkle the onion slices with a little salt and ground black pepper.

8 Pour the chipotle purée onto the chicken breasts, making sure that each piece is evenly coated.

9 Place the casserole in the preheated oven and bake for 45 minutes–1 hour or until the chicken is cooked through, but is still moist and tender. Garnish with fresh oregano and serve with boiled white rice, and *Frijoles de Olla*.

COOK'S TIP

If you are a lover of chipotle chiles, you may wish to use more than six.

TURKEY MOLE

A MOLE IS A RICH STEW, TRADITIONALLY SERVED ON A FESTIVE OCCASION. THE WORD COMES FROM THE AZTEC "MOLLI," MEANING A CHILLI-FLAVORED SAUCE. THERE ARE MANY DIFFERENT TYPES, INCLUDING THE FAMOUS MOLE POBLANO DE GUAJALOTE. TOASTED NUTS, FRUIT AND CHOCOLATE ARE AMONG THE CLASSIC INGREDIENTS; THIS VERSION INCLUDES COCOA POWDER.

SERVES FOUR

INGREDIENTS

1 ancho chile, seeded
1 guajillo chile, seeded
¾ cup sesame seeds
½ cup whole blanched almonds
½ cup shelled unsalted
  peanuts, skinned
1 small onion
2 garlic cloves
¼ cup lard or 4 tablespoons
  vegetable oil
⅓ cup canned tomatoes in
  tomato juice
1 ripe plantain
⅓ cup raisins
½ cup ready-to-eat prunes, pitted
1 teaspoon dried oregano
½ teaspoon ground cloves
½ teaspoon crushed
  allspice berries
1 teaspoon ground cinnamon
¼ cup unsweetened cocoa powder
4 turkey breasts
fresh oregano, to garnish
  (optional)

1 Soak both types of dried chile in a bowl of hot water for 30 minutes, then lift them out and chop them roughly. Reserve 1 cup of the soaking liquid.

COOK'S TIP
It is important to use good quality cocoa powder, which is unsweetened.

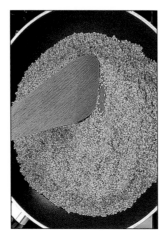

2 Spread out the sesame seeds in a heavy frying pan. Toast them over medium heat, shaking the pan lightly so that they turn golden all over. Do not let them burn, or the sauce will taste bitter. Set aside 3 tablespoons of the toasted seeds for the garnish and put the rest in a bowl. Toast the almonds and peanuts in the same way and add them to the bowl.

3 Chop the onion and garlic finely. Heat half the lard or oil in a frying pan, cook the chopped onion and garlic for 2–3 minutes, then add the chiles and tomatoes. Cook gently for 10 minutes.

4 Peel the plantain and slice it into short diagonal slices. Add it to the onion mixture with the raisins, prunes, dried oregano, spices and cocoa. Stir in the 1 cup of the reserved water in which the chiles were soaked. Bring to a boil, stirring, then add the toasted sesame seeds, almonds and peanuts. Cook for 10 minutes, stirring frequently, then remove from heat and let cool slightly.

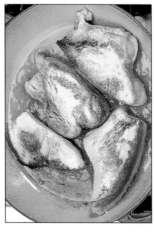

5 Blend the sauce in batches in a food processor or blender until smooth. The sauce should be fairly thick, but a little water may be added if necessary.

6 Heat the remaining lard or oil in a flameproof casserole. Add the turkey and brown over medium heat.

7 Pour the sauce onto the steaks and cover the casserole with aluminum foil and a tight-fitting lid. Cook over low heat for 20–25 minutes or until the turkey is cooked and the sauce has thickened. Sprinkle with sesame seeds and chopped oregano, and serve with a rice dish and warm tortillas.

ENCHILADAS WITH PORK AND GREEN SAUCE

THE GREEN TOMATILLO SAUCE PROVIDES A TART CONTRAST TO THE PORK FILLING IN THIS POPULAR DISH. CASCABELS ARE DRIED CHILES THAT RATTLE WHEN SHAKEN.

SERVES THREE TO FOUR

INGREDIENTS

1¼ pounds pork shoulder, diced
1 cascabel chilli
2 tablespoons oil
2 garlic cloves, crushed
1 onion, finely chopped
scant 2 cups drained
  canned tomatillos
6 fresh corn tortillas
¾ cup grated Monterey Jack or
  mild Cheddar cheese

1 Put the diced pork in a saucepan and pour in water to cover. Bring to a boil, lower the heat and simmer for 40 minutes.

2 Meanwhile, soak the dried chile in hot water for 30 minutes until softened. Drain, remove the stem, then slit the chile and scrape out the seeds.

3 Drain the pork and let it cool slightly, then shred it, using two forks. Put the pork in a bowl and set it aside.

4 Heat the oil in a frying pan and sauté the garlic and onion for 3–4 minutes, until translucent. Chop and add the chile with the tomatillos. Cook, stirring constantly, until the tomatillos start to break up. Lower the heat and simmer the sauce for 10 more minutes. Cool slightly, then purée in a blender.

5 Preheat the oven to 350°F. Soften the tortillas by wrapping them in foil and steaming on a plate over boiling water for a few minutes, until they are pliable. Alternatively, wrap them in microwave-safe plastic wrap and heat in a microwave on full power for about 30 seconds.

6 Spoon one-sixth of the shredded pork onto the center of a tortilla and roll it up to make an enchilada. Place it in a shallow baking dish that is large enough to hold all the enchiladas in a single layer. Fill and roll the remaining tortillas and add them to the dish.

7 Pour the sauce onto the enchiladas to cover completely. Sprinkle evenly with cheese. Bake for 25–30 minutes or until the cheese bubbles. Serve immediately. Tomato salad makes a good accompaniment for this dish.

PORK IN GREEN WITH CACTUS

CHILE VERDE IS A CLASSIC SAUCE OF CACTUS PIECES—A POPULAR INGREDIENT IN MEXICAN COOKING—GIVES THIS CONVERSATION STARTER AT THE ____ G FLAVOR THAT WILL DOUBTLESS PROVE A GOOD

SERVES FOUR

INGREDIENTS
2 tablespoons vegetable oil
1¼ pounds pork shoulder, cut in
    1-inch cubes
1 onion, finely chopped
2 garlic cloves, crushed
1 teaspoon dried oregano
3 fresh jalapeño chiles, seeded
    and chopped
scant 2 cups drained
    canned tomatillos
⅔ cup vegetable stock
11-ounce jar *nopalitos*, drained
salt and ground black pepper
warm fresh corn tortillas, to serve

1 large saucepan. Add
nd cook over high
eral times, until
Add the onion and
gently until soft, then
o and chopped
or 2 more minutes.

3 Meanwhile, soak the *nopalitos* in cold water for 10 minutes. Drain, then add to the pork and continue cooking for about 10 minutes or until the pork is cooked through and tender.

4 Season the mixture with salt and plenty of ground black pepper. Serve with warm corn tortillas.

nned tomatillos to a
stock and process until
he pork mixture, cover
minutes.

COOK'S TIP
Nopalitos are cactus paddles that ha
been cut into strips and pickled in
vinegar or packed in brine. Look for
at specialty food stores.

STUFFED LOIN OF PORK

PORK FEATURES TWICE IN THIS DELICIOUS AND LUXURIOUS DISH, WHICH CONSISTS OF A ROAST LOIN STUFFED WITH A RICH GROUND PORK MIXTURE. THE PERFECT CENTERPIECE FOR A SPECIAL OCCASION DINNER, IT IS SERVED IN MEXICO AT WEDDINGS AND SIMILAR CELEBRATIONS.

SERVES SIX

INGREDIENTS

3–3½ pounds boneless pork loin, butterflied and ready for stuffing

For the stuffing
⅓ cup raisins
½ cup dry white wine
1 tablespoon vegetable oil
1 onion, diced
2 garlic cloves, crushed
½ teaspoon ground cloves
1 teaspoon ground cinnamon
1¼ pounds ground pork
⅔ cup vegetable stock
2 tomatoes
½ cup chopped almonds
½ teaspoon each salt and ground black pepper

1 Make the stuffing. Put the raisins and wine in a bowl. Set aside. Heat the oil in a large pan, add the onion and garlic and cook for 5 minutes over low heat.

2 Add the cloves and cinnamon, then the pork. Cook, stirring, until the pork has browned. Add the stock. Simmer, stirring frequently, for 20 minutes.

3 While the pork is simmering, peel the tomatoes. Cut a cross in the bottom of each tomato, then put them both in a heatproof bowl. Pour in boiling water to cover. Leave the tomatoes in the water for 3 minutes, then lift them out on a slotted spoon and plunge them into a bowl of cold water. Drain. The skins will have begun to peel back from the crosses.

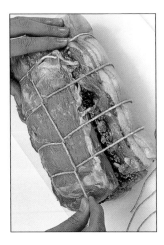

4 Remove the skins completely, then chop the flesh.

5 Stir the tomatoes and almonds into the pork mixture, add the raisins and wine. Cook until the mixture is reduced to a thick sauce. Let cool.

6 Preheat the oven to 350°F. Open out the pork loin and trim it neatly. Season the pork stuffing with salt and pepper to taste. Spread on the surface of the meat in a neat layer, taking it right to the edges and keeping it as even as possible.

7 Roll up the pork loin carefully and tie it at intervals with kitchen string. Weigh the pork and calculate the cooking time at 30 minutes per pound, plus another 30 minutes.

8 Put the stuffed pork joint in a roasting pan, season with salt and pepper and roast for the calculated time. When the joint is cooked, transfer it to a meat platter, place a tent of aluminum foil over it, and let it stand for 10 minutes before carving and serving with the roast vegetables of your choice.

COOK'S TIP
Your butcher will prepare the pork loin for you, if you give plenty of notice.

CARNITAS

SUCCULENT LITTLE PIECES OF MEAT (USUALLY PORK), CARNITAS, LITERALLY "LITTLE MEATS," CAN BE EATEN AS PART OF A MAIN DISH OR USED TO FILL TACOS OR BURRITOS. THEY ARE ALSO SERVED WITH SALSA AS SNACKS OR ANTOJITOS (NIBBLES).

SERVES EIGHT AS AN APPETIZER,
SIX AS A MAIN COURSE

INGREDIENTS

2 dried bay leaves
2 teaspoons dried thyme
1 teaspoon dried marjoram
3–3½ pounds mixed boneless pork
 (loin and leg)
3 garlic cloves
½ teaspoon salt
scant 1 cup lard
1 orange, cut into 8 wedges
1 small onion, thickly sliced
warm flour tortillas, to serve

For the salsa

small bunch of cilantro
1 white onion
8–10 pickled jalapeño chile slices
3 tablespoons freshly squeezed
 orange juice

5 Heat the lard in a flame-proof casserole. Add the pork mixture, with the oranges, garlic cloves and onion. Brown the pork cubes on all sides.

6 Using a slotted spoon, lift out the onion and garlic and discard. Cover the casserole and continue to cook over low heat for about 1½ hours.

7 Remove the lid and lift out and discard the orange wedges. Continue to cook the mixture, uncovered, until all the meat juices have been absorbed and the pork cubes are crisp on the outside and tender and moist inside. Serve with warm tortillas and the salsa.

1 Crumble the bay leaves into a mortar. Add the dried thyme and dried marjoram and grind the mixture with a pestle to a fine powder.

2 Cut the pork into 2-inch cubes and place it in a nonmetallic bowl. Add the herbs and salt. Using your fingers, rub the spice mixture into the meat. Cover and marinate for at least 2 hours, preferably overnight.

3 To make the salsa, remove the stems from the cilantro and chop the leaves roughly. Cut the onion in half, then slice each half thinly. Finely chop the jalapeño chile slices.

4 Mix all the salsa ingredients in a bowl, pour in the freshly squeezed orange juice and toss gently to mix. Cover and chill until needed.

COOK'S TIP

If the *carnitas* are to be served in tacos or burritos, shred or chop them. Make the chunks about half the given size if serving them as *antojitos*. Reduce the cooking time accordingly.

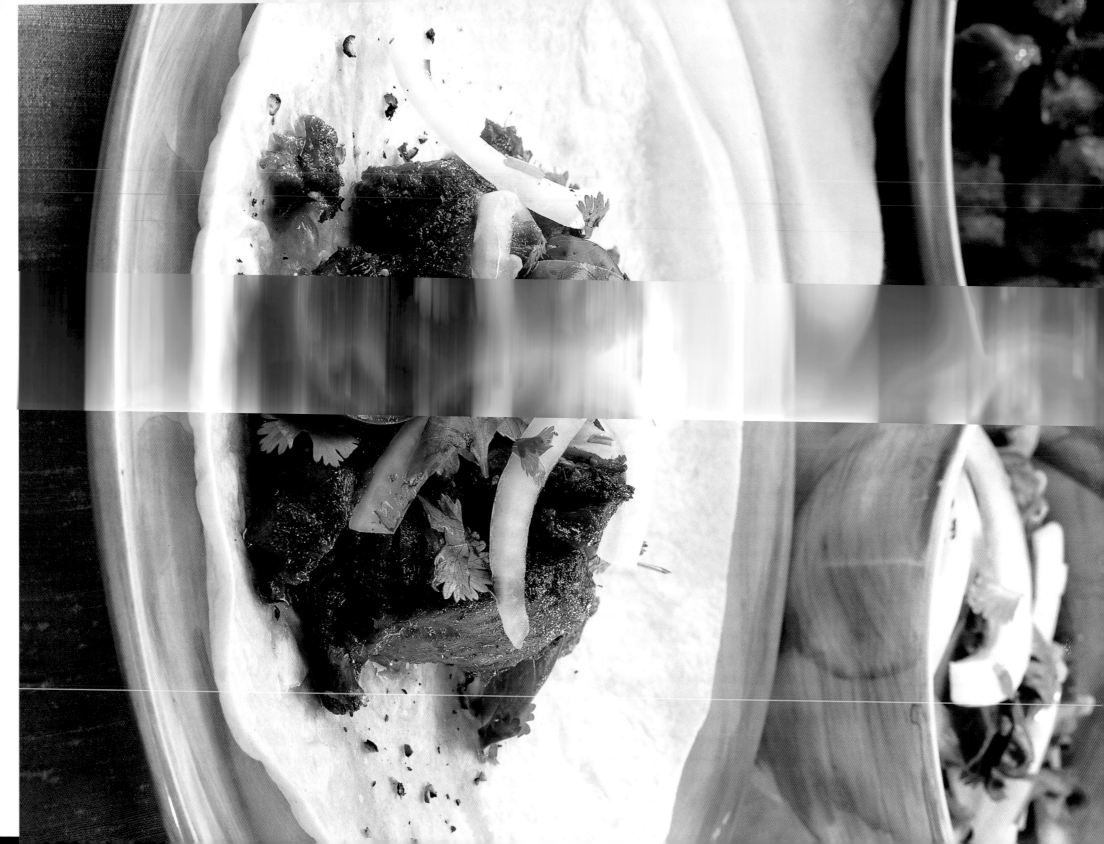

TAMALES FILLED WITH SPICED PORK

These tamales are among the most ancient of Mexican foods. At one time the neat little corn husk parcels filled with plain, savory or sweet masa dough were cooked in the ashes of a wood fire. Today they are more likely to be steamed, but the thrill of unwrapping them remains the same.

SERVES SIX

INGREDIENTS

1¼ pounds lean pork, cut into
    2-inch cubes
3 cups chicken stock
4½ cups *masa harina*
2 cups lard, softened
2 tablespoons salt
12 large or 24 small dried corn husks
2 ancho chiles, seeded
1 tablespoon vegetable oil
½ onion, finely chopped
2–3 garlic cloves, crushed
½ teaspoon allspice berries
2 dried bay leaves
½ teaspoon ground cumin
lime wedges, to serve (optional)

1 Put the pork cubes in a large saucepan. Pour in water to cover. Bring to a boil, lower the heat and simmer for 40 minutes.

2 Meanwhile, heat the chicken stock in a separate pan. Put the *masa harina* in a large bowl and add the hot stock, a little at a time, to make a stiff dough.

3 Put the lard in another bowl and beat with an electric whisk until light and fluffy, as when beating butter for a cake. Test by dropping a small amount of the whipped lard into a cup of water. If it floats, it is ready for use.

4 Continue to beat the lard, gradually adding the *masa* dough. When all of it has been added and the mixture is light and spreadable, beat in the salt. Cover closely with plastic wrap to prevent the mixture from drying out.

5 Put the corn husks in a bowl and pour in boiling water to cover. Let soak for 30 minutes. Soak the seeded chiles in a separate bowl of hot water for the same time. Drain the pork, reserving 7 tablespoons of the cooking liquid, and chop the meat finely.

6 Heat the oil in a large saucepan and fry the onion and garlic over medium heat for 2–3 minutes. Drain the chiles, chop them finely and add them to the pan. Put the allspice berries and bay leaves in a mortar, grind them with a pestle, then work in the ground cumin. Add to the onion mixture and stir well. Cook for 2–3 more minutes. Add the chopped pork and reserved cooking liquid and continue cooking over medium heat until all the liquid is absorbed. Let cool slightly.

7 Drain the corn husks and pat them dry in a clean dish towel. Place one large corn husk (or overlap two smaller ones) on a board. Spoon about one-twelfth of the *masa* mixture onto the center of the husk wrapping and spread it almost to the sides.

8 Place a spoonful of the meat mixture on top of the *masa*. Fold the two long sides of the corn husk over the filling, then bring up each of the two shorter sides in turn, to make a neat parcel. Slide one of the two short sides inside the other, if possible, to prevent the parcel from unravelling, or tie with string or strips of the corn husk.

9 Place the *tamales* in a steamer basket over a pan of steadily simmering water and steam for 1 hour, adding water as needed. To test if the *tamales* are ready, unwrap one. The filling should separate from the husk cleanly. Pile the *tamales* on a plate, let stand for 10 minutes, then serve with lime wedges, if desired. Guests unwrap their own *tamales* at the table.

TACOS WITH SHREDDED BEEF

In Mexico tacos are most often made with soft corn tortillas, which are filled and folded in half. It is unusual to see the crisp shells that are so widely used in Tex-Mex cooking. Tacos are always eaten with the hands.

SERVES SIX

INGREDIENTS

1 pound rump steak, diced
1 cup *masa harina*
½ teaspoon salt
½ cup warm water
2 teaspoons dried oregano
1 teaspoon ground cumin
2 tablespoons oil
1 onion, thinly sliced
2 garlic cloves, crushed
shredded lettuce, lime wedges and
Classic Tomato Salsa, to serve
cilantro, to garnish

1 Put the steak in a deep frying pan and pour in water to cover. Bring to a boil, then lower the heat and simmer for 1–1½ hours.

2 Meanwhile, make the tortilla dough. Mix the *masa harina* and salt in a large mixing bowl. Add the warm water, a little at a time, to make a dough that can be worked into a ball. Knead the dough on a lightly floured surface for 3–4 minutes, until smooth, then wrap the dough in plastic wrap and let rest for 1 hour.

3 Put the meat on a board, let it cool slightly, then shred it, using two forks. Put the meat in a bowl. Divide the tortilla dough into six equal balls.

4 Open a tortilla press and line both sides with plastic (this can be cut from a new plastic sandwich bag). Put each ball on the press and flatten it into a 6–8-inch round.

5 Heat a griddle or frying pan until hot. Cook each tortilla for 15–20 seconds on each side, and then for another 15 minutes on the first side. Keep the tortillas warm and soft by folding them inside a slightly damp dish towel.

6 Add the oregano and cumin to the shredded meat and mix well. Heat the oil in a frying pan and sauté the onion and garlic for 3–4 minutes, until softened. Add the spiced meat mixture and toss over the heat until heated through.

7 Place some shredded lettuce on a tortilla, top with shredded beef and salsa, fold in half and serve with lime wedges. Garnish with cilantro.

BEEF ENCHILA... RED SAUCE

ENCHILADAS ARE USUALLY MADE ...IS, ALTHOUGH IN PARTS OF NORTHERN MEXICO FLOUR TORTILLAS ARE SOMETIMES...

SERVES THREE TO FOUR

INGREDIENTS

1¼ pounds rump steak, cut into 2-inch cubes
2 ancho chiles, seeded
2 pasilla chiles, seeded
2 garlic cloves, crushed
2 teaspoons dried oregano
½ teaspoon ground cumin
2 tablespoons vegetable oil
7 fresh corn tortillas
shredded onion and flat-leaved parsley to garnish
Mango Salsa, to serve

1 Put the steak in a deep frying pan and cover with water. Bring to a boil, then lower the heat and simmer for 1–1½ hours or until very tender.

...ied chiles in a
...t water. Let soak
... the contents of
...d whizz into a
...t cool, reserving
...id. Meanwhile,
...d cumin in the

...d the reserved
...ef. Tear one
...ieces and add
... a boil, then
... 10 minutes,
...he sauce has
..., using two
...uce, heat
...

5 Spoon some of the meat mixture onto each tortilla and roll it up to make an enchilada. Keep the enchiladas in a warmed dish until you have rolled them all. Garnish with shreds of onion and fresh flat-leaved parsley and then serve immediately with the Mango Salsa.

VARIATION

For a richer version, place the rolled enchiladas side by side in a gratin dish. Pour on 1¼ cups sour cream and ¾ cup grated Cheddar cheese. Place under a preheated broiler for 5 minutes or until the cheese melts and the sauce begins to bubble. Serve immediately, with the salsa.

STUFFED BEEF WITH CHEESE AND CHILI SAUCE

THIS RECIPE HAS ITS ORIGINS IN NORTHERN MEXICO, WHICH IS BEEF COUNTRY. IT IS A GOOD WAY TO COOK STEAKS, EITHER UNDER THE BROILER OR ON THE GRILL.

SERVES FOUR

INGREDIENTS

4 fresh serrano chiles
½ cup full-fat soft cheese
2 tablespoons reposada tequila
2 tablespoons oil
1 onion
2 garlic cloves
1 teaspoon dried oregano
½ teaspoon salt
½ teaspoon ground black pepper
1½ cups grated Cheddar cheese
4 fillet steaks, at least
    1 inch thick

6 Cut each steak almost but not quite in half across its width, so that it can be opened out, butterfly-style. Preheat the broiler to its highest setting.

7 Spoon a quarter of the cheese and onion filling on one side of each steak and close the other side over it. Place the steaks in a broiler pan and broil for 3–5 minutes on each side, depending on how you like your steak. Serve on heated plates with the vegetables of your choice, and with the cheese and chili sauce poured on top.

COOK'S TIP

One of the easiest ways of testing whether a steak is cooked is by touch. A steak that is very rare or "blue" will feel soft to the touch; the meat will be relaxed. A rare steak will feel like a sponge, and will spring back when lightly pressed. A medium-rare steak offers more resistance, while a well-cooked steak will feel very firm.

3 Put the cream cheese in a small heavy saucepan and stir over low heat until it has melted. Add the chili strips and the tequila and stir to make a smooth sauce. Keep warm over very low heat.

4 Heat the oil in a frying pan and sauté the onion, garlic and oregano for about 5 minutes over medium heat, stirring frequently, until the onion has browned. Season with the salt and pepper.

5 Remove the pan from heat and stir in the grated cheese so that it melts into the onion mixture.

1 Dry-roast the chiles in a griddle over medium heat, turning them frequently, until the skins are blistered but not burnt. Put them in a strong plastic bag and tie the top to keep the steam in. Set aside for 20 minutes.

2 Remove the chilies from the bag, slit them and scrape out the seeds with a sharp knife. Cut the flesh into long narrow strips, then cut each strip into several shorter strips.

Mexico's delicio... aps the country's best-kept secret. Asked to name the ten most popular M... ople would suggest seafood, yet the Pacific Ocean and the waters of the ... ening with fish, and Mexican cooks put the bounty to excellent use. ... pper and sea bass are just some of the varieties available ... ge succulent shrimp are a specialty, and crabs, crayfish and lobster are also available.

...eviche, which requires no cooking at all, and Escabeche, ...involves frying fish and then marinating it for 24 hours, ...re a host of easy-to-cook dishes that take very little time to ...pare. Some of these, such as Shrimp in Garlic Butter or ...with Garlic and Cilantro, make simple but delicious after- ...while others, such as Baked Salmon with Guava Sauce, ...re elaborate and are perfect for entertaining.

ESCABECHE

A CLASSIC DISH THAT THE MEXICANS INHERITED FROM THE SPANISH, ESCABECHE IS OFTEN CONFUSED WITH CEVICHE, WHICH CONSISTS OF MARINATED RAW FISH. IN ESCABECHE, THE RAW FISH IS INITIALLY MARINATED IN LIME JUICE, BUT IS THEN COOKED BEFORE BEING PICKLED.

SERVES FOUR

INGREDIENTS

2 pounds whole fish fillets

juice of 2 limes

1¼ cups olive oil

6 peppercorns

3 garlic cloves, sliced

½ teaspoon ground cumin

½ teaspoon dried oregano

2 bay leaves

⅓ cup pickled jalapeño chile slices, chopped

1 onion, thinly sliced

1 cup white wine vinegar

1¼ cups green olives stuffed with pimiento, to garnish

1 Place the fish fillets in a single layer in a shallow nonmetallic dish. Pour on the lime juice, turn the fillets over once to ensure that they are completely coated, then cover the dish and let marinate for 15 minutes.

2 Drain the fish in a colander, then pat the fillets dry with paper towels. Heat 4 tablespoons of the oil in a large frying pan, add the fish fillets and sauté for 5–6 minutes, turning once, until they are golden brown. Use a spatula to transfer them to a shallow dish that will hold them in a single layer.

3 Heat 2 tablespoons of the remaining oil in a frying pan. Add the peppercorns, garlic, ground cumin, oregano, bay leaves and jalapeños, and cook over low heat for 2 minutes, then increase the heat, add the onion slices and vinegar and bring to a boil. Lower the heat and simmer for 4 minutes.

4 Remove the pan from heat and carefully add the remaining oil. Stir well, then pour the mixture onto the fish. Let cool, then cover the dish and marinate for 24 hours in the refrigerator.

5 When you are ready to serve, drain off the liquid and garnish the pickled fish with the stuffed olives. Salad leaves would make a good accompaniment.

COOK'S TIP

Use the largest frying pan you have when cooking the fish. If your pan is too small, it may be necessary to cook them in batches. Do not overcrowd the pan, as they will cook unevenly.

CEVICHE

THIS FAMOUS DISH IS PARTICU_____NG MEXICO'S WESTERN SEABOARD, IN PLACES SUCH AS ACAPULCO. IT CONSISTS O_____ISH, "COOKED" BY THE ACTION OF LIME JUICE.

INGREDIENTS

7 ounces raw peeled shrimp

7 ounces shelled scallops

7 ounces squid, cleaned and cut into serving pieces

7 limes

3 tomatoes

1 small onion

1 ripe avocado

¼ cup chopped fresh oregano, or 2 teaspoons dried

1 teaspoon salt

ground black pepper

fresh oregano sprigs, to garnish

crusty bread and lime wedges, to serve (optional)

1 Spread out the shrimp, scallops squid in a non-metallic bowl. Sque six of the limes and pour the juice the mixed seafood to cover it comp Cover the dish with plastic wrap a aside for 8 hours or overnight.

2 Drain the seafood in a colande remove the excess lime juice, th it dry with paper towels. Place th shrimp, scallops and squid in a

atoes in half, squeeze out en dice the flesh. Cut the then slice it thinly. Cut half lengthwise, remove the then cut the flesh into

4 Add the tomatoes, onion and avocado to the seafood with the oregano and seasoning. Squeeze the remaining lime and pour on the juice. Garnish with oregano and serve, with crusty bread and lime wedges, if desired.

SALT COD FOR CHRISTMAS EVE

This Mexican dish is milder than the similar Spanish dish, Bacaldo a la Vizcaina. It is eaten on Christmas Eve throughout Mexico.

SERVES SIX

INGREDIENTS

1 pound dried salt cod
7 tablespoons extra virgin olive oil
1 onion, halved and thinly sliced
4 garlic cloves, crushed
2 x 14-ounce cans chopped tomatoes in tomato juice
¾ cup slivered almonds
½ cup pickled jalapeño chile slices
1 cup green olives stuffed with pimiento
small bunch of fresh parsley, finely chopped
salt and ground black pepper
fresh flat-leaved parsley, to garnish
crusty bread, to serve

1 Put the cod in a large bowl and pour in enough cold water to cover. Soak for 24 hours, changing the water at least five times during this period.

2 Drain the cod and remove the skin using a large sharp knife. Shred the flesh finely using two forks, and put it into a bowl. Set it aside.

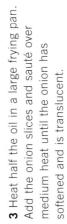

3 Heat half the oil in a large frying pan. Add the onion slices and sauté over medium heat until the onion has softened and is translucent.

4 Remove the onion from the pan and set aside. Make sure you transfer the oil with the onion, as it is an important flavoring in this dish and mustn't be discarded. In the same pan add the remaining olive oil. When the oil is hot but not smoking, add the crushed garlic and sauté gently for 2 minutes.

5 Add the canned tomatoes and their juice to the pan with the garlic. Cook over medium-high heat for about 20 minutes, stirring occasionally, until the mixture has reduced and thickened.

6 Meanwhile, spread out the slivered almonds in a single layer in a large heavy frying pan. Toast them over medium heat for a few minutes, shaking the pan lightly throughout the process so that they turn golden brown all over. Do not let them burn.

7 Add the jalapeño chile slices and stuffed olives to the toasted almonds.

8 Stir in the shredded fish, mixing it in thoroughly, and cook for 20 more minutes, stirring occasionally, until the mixture is almost dry.

9 Season to taste, add the parsley and cook for another 2–3 minutes. Garnish with parsley leaves and serve in heated bowls, with crusty bread.

COOK'S TIPS

• Salt cod is available at specialty fishmongers, Spanish delicatessens and West Indian stores.
• Any leftovers can be used to fill burritos or empanadas.

FRIED SOLE WITH LIME

Simple fish dishes like this one capitalize on the delicious flavor of good fresh fish.

SERVES FOUR

INGREDIENTS

¾ cup all-purpose flour
2 teaspoons garlic salt
1 teaspoon ground black pepper
4 sole fillets
oil, for frying
juice of 2 limes
small bunch of fresh parsley,
　chopped, plus extra sprigs,
　to garnish
fresh salsa, to serve

COOK'S TIP

Make sure the oil is hot enough when
you add the fish, or it will be absorbed
by the fish and the dish will be
too greasy.

1 Combine the flour, garlic salt and
pepper. Spread out the seasoned flour
mixture in a shallow dish. Pat the sole
fillets dry with paper towels, then turn
them in the seasoned flour until they
are evenly coated.

2 Pour oil into a wide frying pan to a
depth of ½ inch. Heat it until a cube
of bread added to the oil rises to the
surface and browns in 45–60 seconds.

3 Add the fish, in batches if necessary,
and fry for 3–4 minutes. Lift each fillet
out and drain it on paper towels.
Transfer to a heated serving dish.

4 Squeeze the juice of half a lime onto
each piece of fish and sprinkle with the
chopped parsley. Serve immediately,
with a fresh salsa to complement the
fish. Garnish with parsley sprigs. New
potatoes would also go well.

BAKED SALMON WITH GUAVA SAUCE

*Guavas have a creamy flesh with a slight citrus tang, which makes them the perfect fruit
for a sauce to serve with salmon. The sauce works well with other fish and is also good
with chicken or turkey.*

SERVES FOUR

INGREDIENTS

6 ripe guavas
3 tablespoons vegetable oil
1 small onion, finely chopped
½ cup well-flavored chicken stock
2 teaspoons hot pepper sauce
4 salmon steaks
salt and ground black pepper
strips of red bell pepper to garnish

COOK'S TIP

Ripe guavas have yellow skin and
succulent flesh that ranges in color from
white to deep pink or salmon red. They
are exceptionally rich in vitamin C. Ripe
fruit will keep in the refrigerator for a
few days; green guavas will need to be
placed in a warm spot until they ripen.

1 Cut each guava in half. Scoop the
seeded soft flesh into a sieve placed
over a bowl. Press it through the sieve,
discard the seeds and skin and set the
pulp aside.

2 Heat 2 tablespoons of the oil in a
frying pan. Sauté the chopped onion for
about 4 minutes over medium heat until
softened and turned translucent.

3 Stir in the guava pulp, with the
chicken stock and hot pepper sauce.
Cook, stirring constantly, until the sauce
thickens. Keep it warm until needed.

4 Brush the salmon steaks on one side
with a little of the remaining oil. Season
them with salt and pepper. Heat a
griddle or ridged pan until very hot and
add the salmon steaks, oiled side down.
Cook for 2–3 minutes, until the
underside is golden, then brush the
surface with oil, turn each salmon steak
over and cook the other side until the
fish is cooked and flakes easily when
tested with the tip of a sharp knife.

5 Transfer each steak to a warmed
plate. Serve, garnished with strips of red
pepper on a pool of sauce. A fresh
green salad is a good accompaniment.

SALMON WITH TEQUILA CREAM SAUCE

Use reposada tequila, which is lightly aged, for this sauce. It has a smoother, more rounded flavor, which goes well with the cream.

SERVES FOUR

INGREDIENTS

3 fresh jalapeño chillies
3 tablespoons olive oil
1 small onion, finely chopped
⅔ cup fish stock
grated rind and juice of 1 lime
½ cup light cream
2 tablespoons reposada tequila
1 firm avocado
4 salmon fillets
salt and ground white pepper
strips of green bell pepper and fresh
  flat-leaved parsley to garnish

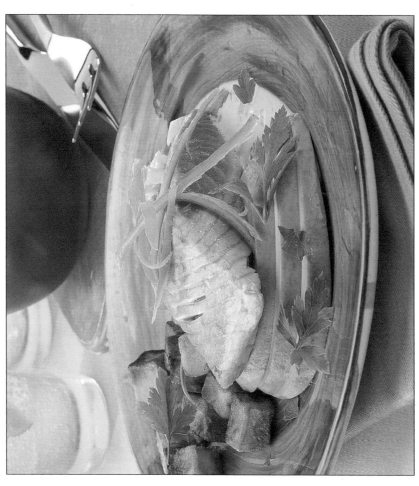

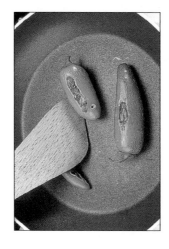

1 Roast the chiles in a frying pan until the skins are blistered, being careful not to let the flesh burn. Put them in a strong plastic bag and tie the top to keep the steam in. Set aside for 20 minutes.

2 Heat 1 tablespoon of the oil in a saucepan. Add the onion and sauté for 3–4 minutes, then add the stock, lime rind and juice. Cook for 10 minutes, until the stock starts to reduce. Remove the chiles from the bag and peel off the skins, slit and scrape out the seeds.

3 Stir the cream into the onion and stock mixture. Slice the chile flesh into strips and add to the pan. Cook over low heat, stirring constantly, for 2–3 minutes. Season to taste with salt and white pepper.

4 Stir the tequila into the onion and chilli mixture. Leave the pan over very low heat. Peel the avocado, remove the pit and slice the flesh. Brush the salmon fillets on one side with a little of the remaining oil.

5 Heat a frying pan or ridged pan until very hot and add the salmon, oiled side down. Cook for 2–3 minutes, until the underside is golden, then brush the top with oil, turn each fillet over and cook the other side until the fish is cooked and flakes easily when tested with the tip of a sharp knife.

6 Serve on a pool of sauce, with the avocado slices. Garnish with strips of green pepper and fresh parsley This is good with Fried Potatoes.

YUCATAN-ST———RK STEAK

A FIRM-FLESHED FISH, SHARK————E, EITHER FRESH OR FROZEN. IT NEEDS CAREFUL WATCHING, AS OVERCOOKING———IND TOUGH, BUT THE FLAVOR IS EXCELLENT.

SERVES FOUR

INGREDIENTS

grated zest and juice of 1 orange
juice of 1 small lime
3 tablespoons white wine
2 tablespoons olive oil
2 garlic cloves, crushed
2 teaspoons ground achiote seed
(annatto powder)
½ teaspoon cayenne pepper
½ teaspoon dried marjoram
1 teaspoon salt
4 shark steaks
fresh oregano leaves, to garnish
4 flour tortillas and any suitable
salsa, to serve

COOK'S TIP
Shark freezes successfully, with little
no loss of flavor on thawing, so use
frozen steaks if you can't find fresh.

zest and juice in a
ic dish which is large
the shark steaks in a
he lime juice, white
lic, ground achiote
cayenne, marjoram

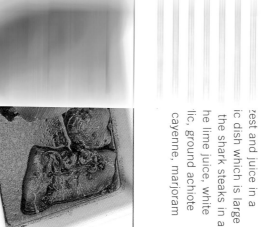

steaks to the dish and
de on them. Cover and
ur, turning once.

3 Heat a griddle until very hot and
cook the marinated shark steaks for
2–3 minutes on each side. Alternatively,
they are very good cooked on the grill,
as long as they are cooked after the
coals have lost their fierce initial heat.
Do not overcook.

4 Garnish the shark steaks with oregano
and serve with the tortillas and salsa. A
green vegetable would also go well.

SWORDFISH TACOS

IT IS IMPORTANT NOT TO OVERCOOK SWORDFISH, OR IT CAN BE TOUGH AND DRY. COOKED CORRECTLY, HOWEVER, IT IS ABSOLUTELY DELICIOUS AND MAKES A GREAT CHANGE FROM BEEF OR CHICKEN AS A TACO FILLING.

SERVES SIX

INGREDIENTS

3 swordfish steaks
2 tablespoons vegetable oil
2 garlic cloves, crushed
1 small onion, chopped
3 fresh green chiles, seeded and chopped
3 tomatoes
small bunch cilantro, chopped
6 fresh corn tortillas
½ iceberg lettuce, shredded
salt and ground black pepper
lemon wedges, to serve (optional)

1 Preheat the broiler. Put the swordfish on an oiled rack over a broiler pan and broil for 2–3 minutes on each side. When cool enough to handle, remove the skin and flake the fish into a bowl.

2 Heat the oil in a saucepan. Add the garlic, onion and chiles and sauté for 5 minutes or until the onion is soft and translucent.

3 Cut a cross in the bottom of each tomato and pour in boiling water. After 3 minutes plunge into cold water. Remove the skins and seeds and chop the flesh into ½ inch dice.

4 Add the tomatoes and swordfish to the onion mixture. Cook for 5 minutes over low heat. Add the cilantro and cook for 1–2 minutes. Season to taste.

5 Wrap the tortillas in foil and steam on a plate over boiling water until pliable. Place some shredded lettuce and fish mixture on each tortilla. Fold in half and serve with lemon wedges, if desired.

GRILLED SWORDFISH WITH CHILI AND LIME SAUCE

SWORDFISH IS A PRIME CANDIDATE FOR THE GRILL, AS LONG AS IT IS NOT OVERCOOKED. IT TASTES WONDERFUL WITH A SPICY SAUCE WHOSE FIRE IS TEMPERED WITH CRÈME FRAÎCHE.

SERVES FOUR

INGREDIENTS

2 fresh serrano chiles
4 tomatoes
3 tablespoons olive oil
grated zest and juice of 1 lime
4 swordfish steaks
½ teaspoon salt
½ teaspoon ground black pepper
¾ cup crème fraîche
fresh flat-leaved parsley to garnish

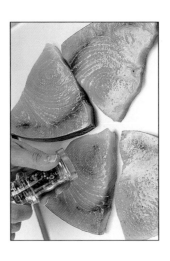

1 Roast the chiles in a dry griddle until the skins are blistered. Put in a strong plastic bag and tie the top. Set aside for 20 minutes, then peel off the skins. Cut off the stalks, then slit the chiles, scrape out the seeds and slice the flesh.

2 Cut a cross in the bottom of each tomato. Place them in a heatproof bowl and pour in boiling water to cover. After 3 minutes, lift the tomatoes out on a slotted spoon and plunge them into a bowl of cold water. Drain. The skins will have begun to peel back from the crosses. Remove all the skin from the tomatoes, then cut them in half and squeeze out the seeds. Chop the flesh into ½-inch pieces.

3 Heat 1 tablespoon of the oil in a small saucepan and add the strips of chile, with the lime zest and juice. Cook for 2–3 minutes, then stir in the tomatoes. Cook for 10 minutes, stirring the mixture occasionally, until the tomato is pulpy.

4 Brush the swordfish steaks with olive oil and season. Grill for 3–4 minutes or until just cooked, turning once. Meanwhile, stir the crème fraîche into the sauce, heat it through gently and pour onto the swordfish steaks. Serve garnished with fresh parsley. Grill some vegetables as well.

SHRIMP WITH ALMOND SAUCE

GROUND ALMONDS ADD AN INTERESTING TEXTURE TO THE CREAMY, PIQUANT SAUCE THAT ACCOMPANIES THESE SHRIMP.

SERVES SIX

INGREDIENTS

1 ancho or similar dried chile
2 tablespoons vegetable oil
1 onion, chopped
3 garlic cloves, roughly chopped
8 tomatoes
1 teaspoon ground cumin
½ cup chicken stock
generous 1 cup
    ground almonds
¾ cup crème fraîche
½ lime
2 pounds cooked peeled prawns
salt
cilantro and scallion strips,
    to garnish
cooked rice and warm tortillas,
    to serve

1 Place the dried chile in a heatproof bowl and pour in boiling water to cover. Let soak for 30 minutes until softened. Drain, remove the stem, then slit the chile and scrape out the seeds with a small sharp knife. Chop the flesh roughly and set it aside.

2 Heat the oil in a frying pan and sauté the onion and garlic until soft.

VARIATIONS
Try this sauce with other types of fish, too. Adding just a few shrimp and serving it over steamed sole would make a very luxurious dish. The sauce is also very good with chicken.

6 Pour the mixture into a large saucepan, add the ground almonds and stir over low heat for 2–3 minutes. Stir in the crème fraîche until it has been incorporated completely.

3 Cut a cross in the bottom of each tomato. Place them in a heatproof bowl and pour in boiling water to cover. After 3 minutes, lift the tomatoes out on a slotted spoon and plunge them into a bowl of cold water. Drain. The skins will have begun to peel off.

4 Skin the tomatoes completely, then cut them in half and scoop out the seeds. Chop the flesh into ½-inch cubes and add it to the onion mixture, with the chopped chile. Stir in the ground cumin and cook for 10 minutes, stirring occasionally.

7 Squeeze the juice from the lime and stir it into the sauce. Season with salt to taste, then increase the heat and bring the sauce to the simmering point.

5 Put the mixture in a food processor or blender. Add the stock and process on high speed until smooth.

8 Add the shrimp and heat for 2–3 minutes, depending on size, until warmed through. Serve on a bed of rice and pass warm tortillas separately.

SHRIMP IN GARLIC BUTTER

THIS QUICK AND EASY DISH IS PERFECT FOR SERVING TO FRIENDS WHO DON'T MIND GETTING THEIR HANDS DIRTY. PROVIDE A PLATE FOR THE SHRIMP SHELLS AND PASS WARM TORTILLAS FOR MOPPING UP THE DELECTABLE JUICES.

SERVES SIX

INGREDIENTS

2 pounds large jumbo shrimp, in their shells, thawed if frozen
½ cup butter
1 tablespoon vegetable oil
6 garlic cloves, crushed
grated zest and juice of 2 limes
small bunch of cilantro, chopped
warm tortillas, to serve
lemon slices, for the finger bowls

1 Rinse the shrimp in a colander, remove their heads and let them drain. Heat the butter and oil in a large frying pan, add the garlic and sauté over low heat for 2–3 minutes.

2 Add the lime zest and juice. Cook, stirring constantly, for 1 more minute.

COOK'S TIP

Cook the shrimp in a large frying pan or cast iron flameproof dish that can be taken directly to the table, so that they retain their heat until they are served.

3 Add the shrimp and cook them for 2–3 minutes, until they turn pink. Remove from heat, sprinkle with cilantro and serve with the warm tortillas. Give each guest a finger bowl filled with water and a slice of lemon, for cleaning their fingers after shelling the shrimp, and provide paper napkins.

SHRIMP SAL

IN MEXICO, THIS SALAD WOU... ...COURSE IN A FORMAL MEAL, BUT IT IS SO GOOD THAT YOU'LL WANT TO SERVE ... ...OCCASIONS. IT IS PERFECT FOR A BUFFET LUNCH.

SERVES FOUR

INGREDIENTS

1 pound cooked peeled shrimp
juice of 1 lime
3 tomatoes
1 ripe but firm avocado
2 tablespoons hot chili sauce
1 teaspoon sugar
⅔ cup sour cream
2 Boston lettuces, separated into leaves
salt and ground black pepper
fresh basil leaves and strips of green bell pepper to garnish

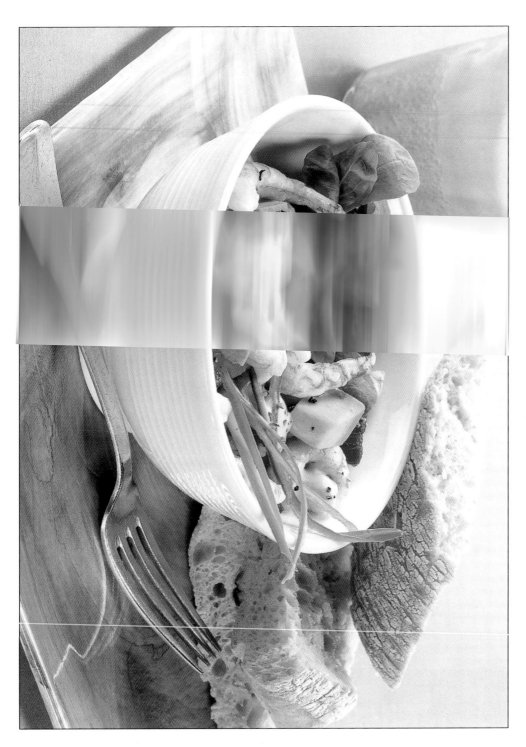

1 Put the shrimp in a large bowl, ac... the lime juice and salt and pepper. lightly, then leave to marinate.

...ne bottom of each
...m in a heatproof bowl
...g water to cover.

..., lift the tomatoes out
...n and plunge them
...d water. Drain. The
...gun to peel back
...osses.

...bes completely, then
...and squeeze out the
...flesh into ½-inch cubes
...shrimp.

...lo in half, remove the
...n slice the flesh into
...Add it to the shrimp
...ure.

6 Mix the hot chili sauce, sugar and sour cream in a bowl. Fold into the shrimp mixture. Line a bowl with the lettuce leaves, then top with the shrimp mixture. Cover and chill for at least 1 hour, then garnish with fresh basil and strips of green pepper. Crusty bread makes a perfect accompaniment.

PUEBLO BAKED FISH

THE LIME JUICE IS A PERFECT PARTNER FOR THE TROUT, WHICH IS AN OILY FISH. MARINATING MEANS THAT THE FISH IS BEAUTIFULLY TENDER WHEN COOKED.

SERVES FOUR

INGREDIENTS

2 fresh pasilla chiles
4 rainbow trout, cleaned
4 garlic cloves
2 teaspoons dried oregano
juice of 2 limes
1½ cup slivered almonds
salt and ground black pepper

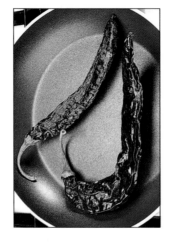

1 Roast the chiles in a dry frying pan or griddle until the skins are blistered, being careful not to let the flesh burn. Put them in a strong plastic bag and tie the top to keep the steam in. Set aside for 20 minutes.

3 Remove the chiles from the bag and peel off the skins. Cut off the stems, then slit the chiles and scrape out the seeds. Chop the flesh roughly and put it in a mortar. Crush with a pestle until the mixture forms a paste.

4 Place the chili paste in a shallow dish that will hold all the trout in a single layer. Slice the garlic lengthwise and add to the dish.

5 Add the oregano and 2 teaspoons salt, then stir in the lime juice and pepper to taste. Add the trout, turning to coat them in the mixture. Cover the dish and set aside for at least 30 minutes, turning the trout again halfway through.

7 Place one of the trout on one of the pieces of paper, moisten with the marinade, then sprinkle about a quarter of the almonds on the top.

8 Bring up the sides of the paper and fold over to seal in the fish, then fold the foil over to make a neat parcel. Make three more parcels in the same way, then place them side by side in a large roasting pan.

9 Transfer the parcels to the oven and bake for 25 minutes. Put each parcel on an individual plate, or open them in the kitchen and serve unwrapped if you prefer. This dish goes well with new potatoes and cooked fresh vegetables.

2 Meanwhile, rub a little salt into the cavities in the trout, to ensure that they are completely clean, then rinse them under cold running water. Drain and pat dry with paper towels.

6 Preheat the oven to 400°F. Have ready four pieces of aluminum foil, each large enough to wrap a trout. Top each sheet with a piece of waxed paper of the same size.

COOK'S TIP

Cooking fish in a paper parcel means that it stays very moist. Trout cooks perfectly by this method, but you could use other fish; try tuna steaks, small mackerel or salmon fillets.

FISHERMAN'S STEW

THIS IS JUST THE SORT OF ONE-POT MEAL YOU CAN IMAGINE FISHERMEN COOKING FOR THEMSELVES, USING FRESHLY CAUGHT FISH AND A FEW VEGETABLES.

SERVES SIX

INGREDIENTS

1¼ pounds mussels
3 onions
2 garlic cloves, sliced
1¼ cups fish stock
12 scallops
1 pound cod fillet
2 tablespoons olive oil
1 large potato, about 7 ounces
few sprigs of fresh thyme, chopped
1 red and 1 green bell pepper
½ cup dry white wine
1 cup crème fraîche
10 ounces peeled shrimp
¾ cup grated aged
    Cheddar cheese
salt and ground black pepper
fresh thyme sprigs, to garnish

3 Cook the mussels for 5–6 minutes, shaking the pan occasionally. Remove them as they open, discarding any that remain shut. Remove the mussels from their shells and set them aside.

4 Strain the cooking liquid from the mussels through a muslin-lined sieve to remove any remaining sand. Make up the liquid with fish stock to 1¼ cups.

7 Cut the remaining onions into small wedges. Heat the olive oil in a large saucepan and fry the onion wedges for 2–3 minutes. Slice the potato about ½ inch thick and add to the pan, with the fresh chopped thyme. Cover and cook for about 15 minutes, until the potato has softened.

8 Core the peppers, remove the cores and seeds, then dice the flesh. Add to the onion and potato mixture and cook for a few minutes. Stir in the mixed mussel and fish stock, with the wine and crème fraîche.

9 Bring to just below the boiling point, then add the cod and scallops. Lower the heat and simmer for 5 minutes, then add the shrimp. Simmer for another 3–4 minutes, until all the seafood is cooked. Stir in the mussels and warm through for 1–2 minutes. Season the sauce if necessary. Spoon into bowls, garnish with the thyme sprigs and sprinkle on the cheese. Crusty bread would be an ideal accompaniment.

5 If you have bought scallops in their shells, open them: hold a scallop shell in the palm of your hand, with the flat side facing up. Insert the blade of a knife close to the hinge that joins the shells and prise apart. Run the blade of the knife across the inside of the flat shell to cut off the scallop. Only the white adductor muscle and the orange coral are eaten, so pull off and discard all other parts. Rinse the scallops under cold running water to remove any grit or sand, then put them in a bowl and set them aside.

6 Cut the cod into large cubes and put it in a bowl. Season with salt and pepper and set aside.

1 Clean the mussel shells, removing any beards. Discard any that stay open when tapped. Rinse in cold water.

2 Pour water to a depth of 1 inch into a large, deep frying pan. Chop one onion and add it to the pan, with the sliced garlic. Bring to a boil, then add the mussels and cover the pan tightly.

VEGETABLES

...ards arrived in Mexico they discovered that the indigenous

...a wide range of vegetables including corn, which was

...varieties of squash and pumpkin, avocados, bell peppers

...my of these vegetables have since been introduced into our

...s were brought to England during the reign of Queen

...b I; others, such as jicama, the crisp textured vegetable

...that can be eaten raw or cooked, have been introduced to

our diets through other cuisines such as Chinese.

Many of these dishes could form the basis of a
meal on their own, while side dishes such as green
and yellow rice, fried potatoes, and Mexican-style
green peas will add flavor and color to any meal.

The wide range of recipes in this chapter is testimony
to the great variety of vegetables that are still being eaten
in Mexico today.

MEXICAN-STYLE GREEN PEAS

This is a delicious way of cooking fresh peas, and makes an excellent accompaniment to any meal. The flavor comes from the vegetables themselves, so use ripe tomatoes and organic peas if possible.

<u>SERVES FOUR</u>

INGREDIENTS

2 tomatoes
¼ cup butter
2 garlic cloves, halved
1 medium onion, halved and
   thinly sliced
scant 3 cups shelled
   fresh peas
2 tablespoons water
salt and ground black pepper
fresh chives, to garnish

1 Cut a cross in the bottom of each tomato. Place the tomatoes in a heatproof bowl and pour in boiling water to cover. Leave them in the water for 3 minutes, then lift the tomatoes out on a slotted spoon and plunge them into a bowl of cold water. Drain. The skins will have begun to peel back.

2 Remove the skins completely, then cut the tomatoes in half and squeeze out the seeds. Chop the flesh into ½-inch dice.

3 Melt the butter in a saucepan. Cook the garlic until golden. Do not overcook or it will add a bitter taste. Lift it out on a slotted spoon and discard it. Add the onion slices to the pan and sauté until transparent.

4 Add the tomato to the onion, mix well, then stir in the peas. Pour in the water, lower the heat and cover the pan tightly. Cook for 10 minutes, shaking the pan occasionally to stop the mixture from sticking to the bottom.

5 Check that the peas are cooked, then season with plenty of salt and pepper. Transfer the mixture to a heated dish and serve, garnished with fresh chives.

MUSHROOMS <u>WITH</u> CHIPOTLE CHILES

Chipotle chiles are jalapeños that have been smoke-dried. Their smoky flavor is the perfect foil for the mushrooms in this simple salad.

<u>SERVES SIX</u>

INGREDIENTS

2 chipotle chiles
6 cups button mushrooms
¼ cup vegetable oil
1 onion, finely chopped
2 garlic cloves, crushed or chopped
salt
small bunch of cilantro, to garnish

COOK'S TIP

Baby button mushrooms are perfect for this dish, if you can get them. You can, of course, use any white mushrooms, but larger ones may be better halved or quartered.

1 Soak the dried chiles in a bowl of hot water for about 10 minutes until they are softened. Drain, cut off the stems, then slit the chiles and scrape out the seeds. Chop the flesh finely.

2 Trim the mushrooms, then clean them with a damp cloth or paper towels. If they are large, cut them in half.

3 Heat the oil in a large frying pan. Add the onion, garlic, chiles and mushrooms and stir until evenly coated in the oil. Fry for 6–8 minutes, stirring occasionally, until the onion and mushrooms are tender. Season to taste and spoon into a serving dish. Chop some of the cilantro, leaving some whole leaves, and use to garnish. Serve hot.

STUFFED CHILES IN WALNUT SAUCE

THE POTATO AND MEAT FILLING IN THESE CHILES IS A GOOD PARTNER FOR THE RICH, CREAMY SAUCE THAT COVERS THEM.

SERVES FOUR

INGREDIENTS

8 ancho chillies
1 large potato, about 7 ounces
3 tablespoons vegetable oil
4 ounces lean ground pork
1 onion, chopped
1 teaspoon ground cinnamon
1 cup walnuts, roughly chopped
½ cup chopped almonds
⅔ cup cream cheese
½ cup soft goat cheese
½ cup light cream
½ cup dry sherry
½ cup all-purpose flour
½ teaspoon ground white pepper
2 eggs, separated
oil, for deep-frying
salt
chopped fresh herbs,
to garnish

1 Soak the dried chiles in a bowl of hot water for 30 minutes, until softened. Drain, cut off the stems, then slit them down one side. Scrape out the seeds with a small sharp knife, taking care to keep the chiles intact for stuffing.

2 Peel the potato and cut it into ½-inch cubes. Heat 1 tablespoon of the oil in a large frying pan, add the pork and cook, stirring, until it has browned evenly.

COOK'S TIP

The potatoes must not break or become too floury. Do not overcook. For the best results buy waxy potatoes.

3 Add the potato cubes and mix well. Cover and cook over low heat for 25–30 minutes, stirring occasionally. Do not worry if the potato sticks to the bottom of the pan. Season with salt, remove from heat and set aside.

4 Heat the remaining oil in a separate frying pan and sauté the onion with the cinnamon for 3–4 minutes or until softened. Stir in the nuts and cook for 3–4 more minutes.

5 Add both types of cheese to the pan, with the cream and sherry. Mix well. Reduce the heat to the lowest setting and cook until the cheese melts and the sauce starts to thicken. Taste and season if necessary.

6 Spread out the flour on a plate or in a shallow dish. Season with the white pepper. Beat the egg yolks in a bowl until they are pale and thick.

7 In a separate, greasefree bowl, whisk the whites until they form soft peaks. Add a generous pinch of salt, then fold in the yolks, a little at a time.

8 Spoon some of the filling into each chilli. Pat the outside dry with paper towels. Heat the oil for deep-frying to a temperature of 350°F.

9 Coat a chile in flour, then dip it in the egg batter, covering it completely. Drain for a few seconds, then add to the hot oil. Add several more battered chiles, but do not overcrowd the pan. Fry the chiles until golden, then drain on paper towels and keep hot while cooking successive batches.

10 Reheat the sauce over low heat, if necessary. Arrange the chiles on individual plates, spoon a little sauce on each and serve immediately, sprinkled with chopped fresh herbs. A green salad goes well with this dish.

GREEN LIMA BEANS IN SAUCE

MAKE THE MOST OF LIMA BEANS OR FAVA BEANS BY TEAMING THEM WITH TOMATOES AND FRESH CHILES IN THIS SIMPLE ACCOMPANIMENT.

<u>SERVES FOUR</u>

INGREDIENTS

1 pound fresh lima beans or
   fava beans
2 tablespoons olive oil
1 onion, finely chopped
2 garlic cloves, crushed
14-ounce can plum tomatoes,
   drained and chopped
about 3 tablespoons drained pickled
   jalapeño chilli slices, chopped
salt
cilantro and lemon slices,
   to garnish

COOK'S TIP
Pickled chiles are often hotter than
roasted chiles—taste one before adding to
the recipe and adjust the quantity to suit
your taste.

1 Bring a saucepan of lightly salted
water to a boil. Add the lima beans or
fava beans and cook for 15 minutes
or until just tender.

2 Meanwhile, heat the olive oil in a
frying pan, add the onion and garlic and
sauté until the onion is translucent. Add
the tomatoes and continue to cook,
stirring, until the mixture thickens.

3 Add the chili slices and cook for
1–2 minutes. Season with salt to taste.

4 Drain the beans and return them to
the pan. Pour in the tomato mixture and
stir over the heat for a few minutes. If
the sauce thickens too quickly, add a
little water. Spoon into a serving dish,
garnish with the cilantro and lemon
slices and serve.

GREEN BEANS WITH EGGS

THIS IS AN UNUSUAL WAY OF COOKING GREEN BEANS, BUT TASTES DELICIOUS. TRY THIS DISH FOR A LIGHT SUPPER OR AS AN ACCOMPANIMENT TO A SIMPLE ROAST.

<u>SERVES SIX</u>

INGREDIENTS

11 ounces string beans,
   trimmed and halved
2 tablespoons vegetable oil
1 onion, halved and
   thinly sliced
3 eggs
salt and ground black pepper
½ cup grated Monterey Jack or
   mild Cheddar cheese
strips of lemon zest, to garnish

VARIATION
Freshly grated Parmesan can be used
instead of the Monterey Jack or Cheddar
cheese for a sharper flavor.

1 Bring a saucepan of water to a boil,
add the beans and cook for 5–6 minutes
or until tender. Drain in a colander,
rinse under cold water to preserve the
bright color, then drain the beans
once more.

2 Heat the oil in a frying pan and sauté
the onion slices for 3–4 minutes, until
soft and translucent. Break the eggs into
a bowl and beat them with seasoning.

3 Add the egg mixture to the onion.
Cook slowly over moderate heat, stirring
constantly so that the egg is lightly
scrambled. The egg should be moist
throughout. Do not overcook.

4 Add the beans to the pan and cook
for a few minutes until warmed through.
Transfer the mixture to a heated serving
dish, sprinkle on the grated cheese and
lemon zest and serve.

ZUCCHINI WITH CHEESE AND GREEN CHILES

THIS IS A VERY TASTY WAY TO SERVE ZUCCHINI, OFTEN A RATHER BLAND VEGETABLE, AND THE DISH LOOKS GOOD TOO. SERVE IT AS A VEGETARIAN MAIN DISH OR AN UNUSUAL SIDE DISH.

SERVES SIX AS AN ACCOMPANIMENT

INGREDIENTS

2 tablespoons vegetable oil
½ onion, thinly sliced
2 garlic cloves, crushed
1 teaspoon dried oregano
2 tomatoes
⅓ cup drained pickled jalapeño
   chili slices, chopped
1¼ pounds zucchini
½ cup cream cheese, cubed
salt and ground black pepper
fresh oregano sprigs,
   to garnish

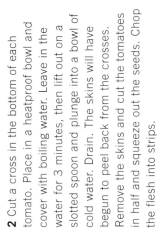

2 Cut a cross in the bottom of each tomato. Place in a heatproof bowl and cover with boiling water. Leave in the water for 3 minutes, then lift out on a slotted spoon and plunge into a bowl of cold water. Drain. The skins will have begun to peel back from the crosses. Remove the skins and cut the tomatoes in half and squeeze out the seeds. Chop the flesh into strips.

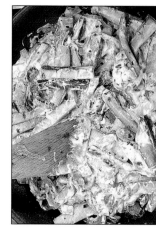

3 Trim the zucchinis then cut them lengthwise into ½ inch wide strips. Slice the strips into matchsticks.

4 Stir the zucchini into the onion mixture and fry for 10 minutes, stirring occasionally, until just tender. Add the tomatoes and chopped jalapeños and cook for 2–3 more minutes.

1 Heat the oil in a frying pan. Add the onion, garlic and dried oregano. Sauté for 3–4 minutes, until the onion is soft and translucent.

5 Add the cream cheese. Reduce the heat to the lowest setting. As the cheese melts, stir gently to coat the zucchini. Season with salt, pile into a heated dish and serve, garnished with fresh oregano. If serving as a main dish, rustic bread makes a good accompaniment.

ZUCCHINI TC

THIS DISH LOOKS LIKE A SPAN ... IS TRADITIONALLY SERVED AT ROOM TEMPERATURE.

SERVE WARM OR PREPARE IT IN ... OOL, BUT DO NOT REFRIGERATE.

SERVES FOUR TO SIX

INGREDIENTS

1¼ pounds zucchini

¼ cup vegetable oil

1 small onion

3 fresh jalapeño chiles, seeded
and cut in strips

3 large eggs

½ cup self-rising flour

1 cup grated Monterey Jack or
mild Cheddar cheese

½ teaspoon cayenne pepper

1 tablespoon butter

salt

2 Slice the onion and add it to the oil remaining in the pan, with most of the jalapeño strips, reserving some for the garnish. Sauté until the onions have softened and are golden. Using a slotted spoon, add the onions and jalapeños to the zucchini.

3 Beat the eggs in a large bowl. Add the self-rising flour, cheese and cayenne. Mix well, then stir in the zucchini mixture, with salt to taste.

350°F. Trim the
m thinly. Heat
pan. Add the
few minutes,
ıst once, until
ıing to brown.
 transfer them

4 Grease a 9-inch round shallow ovenproof dish with the butter. Pour in the zucchini mixture and bake for 30 minutes, until risen, firm to the touch and golden. Let cool.

5 Serve the zucchini torte in thick wedges, garnished with the remaining jalapeño strips. A tomato salad, sprinkled with chives, makes a colorful accompaniment.

PUMPKIN WITH SPICES

ROASTED PUMPKIN HAS A WONDERFUL, RICH FLAVOR. EAT IT STRAIGHT FROM THE SKIN, EAT THE SKIN TOO, OR SCOOP OUT THE COOKED FLESH, ADD A SPOONFUL OF SALSA AND WRAP IT IN A WARM TORTILLA. IT ALSO MAKES FLAVORFUL SOUPS AND SAUCES.

SERVES SIX

INGREDIENTS

2¼ pounds pumpkin
¼ cup butter, melted
2 teaspoons hot chili sauce
½ teaspoon salt
½ teaspoon ground allspice
1 teaspoon ground cinnamon
chopped fresh herbs, to garnish
Classic Tomato Salsa and crème fraîche, to serve

COOK'S TIP

Green, gray or orange-skinned pumpkins all roast well. The orange-fleshed varieties are the most colorful when it comes to cooking.

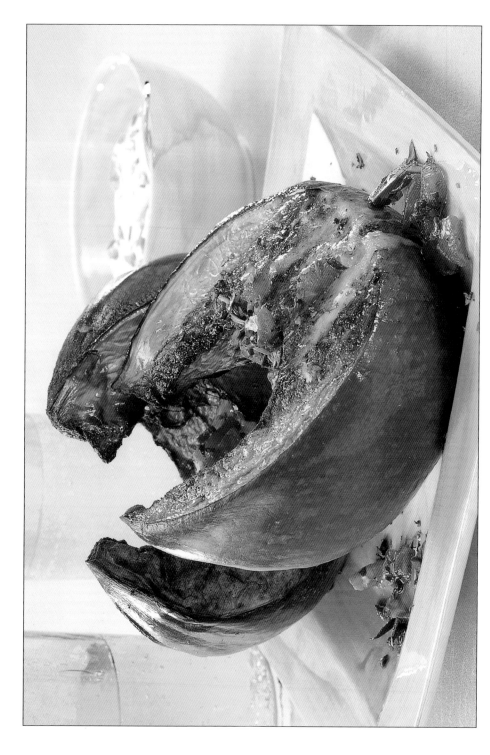

1 Preheat the oven to 425°F. Cut the pumpkin into large pieces. Scoop out and discard the fiber and seeds, then put the pumpkin pieces in a roasting pan.

2 Mix the melted butter and chili sauce and drizzle the mixture evenly on the pumpkin pieces.

3 Put the salt in a small bowl and add the ground allspice and cinnamon. Sprinkle the mixture on the pumpkin.

4 Roast for 25 minutes or until the pumpkin flesh yields when pressed gently. Serve on a heated platter and pass the tomato salsa and crème fraîche separately.

POTATO CAKE

QUICK AND EASY TO MAKE, Th— 1RE DELICIOUS. SERVE THEM WITH SALSA AS A
LIGHT MEAL, OR AS AN ACCOM— OR PAN-FRIED MEATS.

MAKES TEN

INGREDIENTS

1 pound 6 ounces potatoes
1 cup grated Cheddar cheese
½ teaspoon salt
⅓ cup drained pickled jalapeño
  chile slices, finely chopped
  (optional)
1 egg, beaten
small bunch of cilantro,
  finely chopped
all-purpose flour, for shaping
oil, for shallow frying
fresh citrus salsa, to serve

nd halve them if
aucepan of cold
nd cook for about
er. Drain, return
nash. The mixture

2 Scrape the potatoes into a bowl and stir in the grated cheese, with the salt and the chopped jalapeños, if using. Stir in the beaten egg and most of the chopped cilantro and mix into a dough.

3 When the dough is cool enough to handle, put it on a board. With floured hands, divide it into ten pieces of equal size. Shape each piece into a ball, then flatten to a cake.

4 Heat the oil in a large frying par. Fry the potato cakes, in batches if necessary, for 2–3 minutes over medium heat. Turn them over and cook until both sides are golden. Pile on a platter, sprinkle with salt and the remaining chopped cilantro and serve with salsa.

FRIED PLANTAINS

THESE ARE THE PERFECT ACCOMPANIMENT TO HIGHLY SPICED AND SEASONED FOODS. THEIR SWEET FLAVOR PROVIDES AN INTERESTING CONTRAST.

SERVES FOUR

INGREDIENTS
4 ripe plantains
6 tablespoons butter
2 teaspoons vegetable oil
strips of scallion and red bell pepper, to garnish

COOK'S TIP
Ripe plantains have dark, almost black skins. Do not use under-ripe plantains, which are very hard and do not soften on cooking.

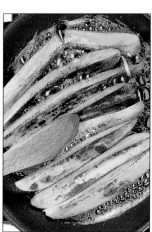

1 Peel the plantains, cut them in half lengthwises, then cut them in half again. Melt the butter with the oil in a large frying pan.

2 Add the plantains to the pan in a single layer and fry for 8–10 minutes, turning halfway through. Spoon into a heated dish and serve, garnished with strips of scallion and red pepper.

FRIED POTATOES

THESE MAKE THE PERFECT ACCOMPANIMENT FOR CHORIZO, AND ALSO GO VERY WELL WITH EGGS AND BACON.

SERVES FOUR

INGREDIENTS
6 fresh jalapeño chiles
4 tablespoons vegetable oil
1 onion, finely chopped
1 pound waxy potatoes, scrubbed and cut in ½-inch cubes
few sprigs of fresh oregano, chopped plus extra sprigs, to garnish
1 cup freshly grated Parmesan cheese (optional)

1 Dry-roast the jalapeños in a griddle pan, turning them frequently so that the skins blacken but do not burn. Place them in a strong plastic bag and tie the top to keep the steam in. Set aside for 20 minutes.

2 Remove the jalapeños from the bag, peel off the skins and remove any stems. Cut them in half, scrape out the seeds, then chop the flesh finely.

COOK'S TIP
If your frying pan does not have a lid, use aluminum foil instead.

3 Meanwhile, heat half the oil in a large heavy frying pan that has a lid. Add the onion and sauté, stirring occasionally, for 3–4 minutes, until translucent, then add the potato cubes.

4 Stir to coat the potato cubes in oil, then cover the pan and cook over medium heat for 20–25 minutes, until the potatoes are tender. Shake the pan occasionally to stop them from sticking to the bottom.

5 When the potatoes are tender, push them to the side of the frying pan, then add the remaining oil.

6 When the oil is hot, spread out the potatoes again and add the chopped jalapeños. Cook over high heat for 5–10 minutes, stirring carefully so that the potatoes turn golden brown all over but do not break up.

7 Add the chopped oregano, with the grated Parmesan, if using. Mix gently, spoon onto a heated serving dish and garnish with extra oregano sprigs. Serve as part of a cooked breakfast or brunch.

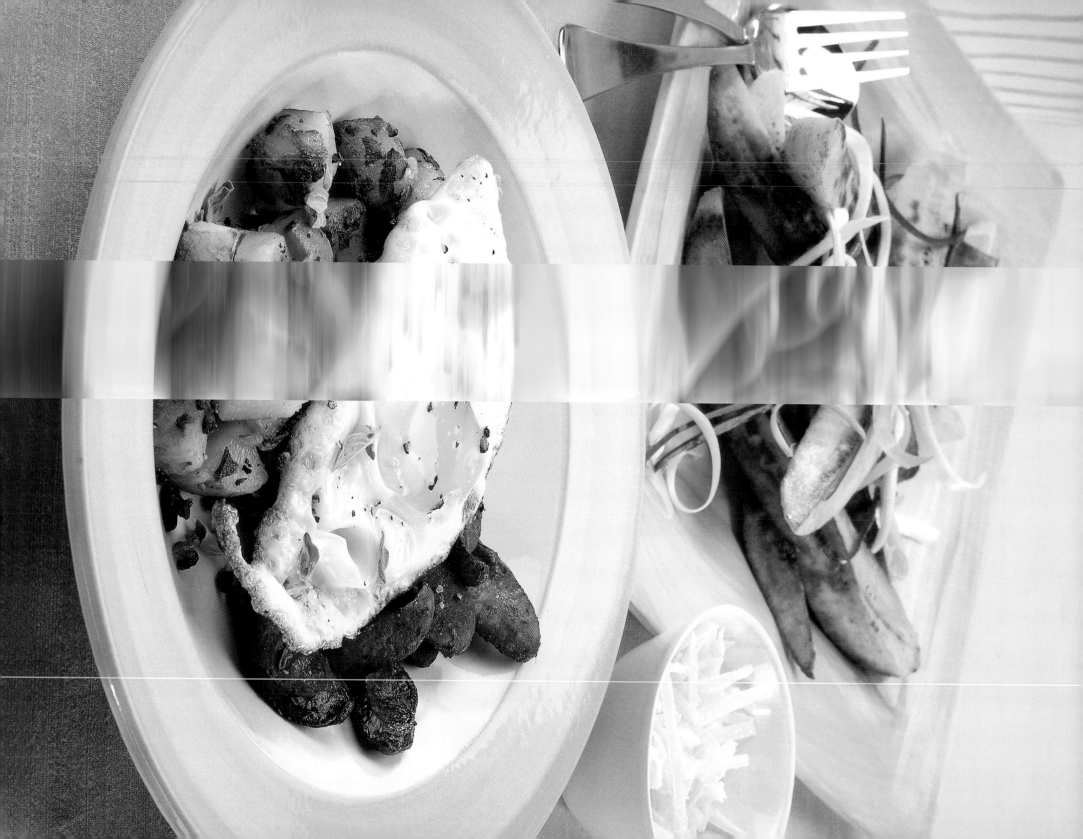

CORN WITH CREAM

IN MEXICO, THIS WOULD BE MADE WITH HEAVY CREAM, BUT THE SAUCE HAS A BETTER CONSISTENCY WHEN MADE WITH CREAM CHEESE.

SERVES SIX AS A SIDE DISH

INGREDIENTS
4 ears of corn
¼ cup butter
1 small onion, finely chopped
⅔ cup drained pickled jalapeño
    chile slices
⅔ cup cream cheese
⅓ cup freshly grated Parmesan
    cheese, plus shavings,
    to garnish
salt and ground black pepper

1 Strip off the husks from the corn and pull off the silks. Place the ears in a bowl of water and use a vegetable brush to remove any remaining silks. Stand each ear in turn on a board and slice off the kernels, cutting as close to the cob as possible.

2 Melt the butter in a saucepan, add the chopped onion and sauté for 4–5 minutes, stirring occasionally, until the onion has softened and is translucent.

3 Add the corn kernels and cook for 4–5 minutes, until they are just tender. Chop the jalapeños finely and stir them into the corn mixture.

4 Stir in the cream cheese and the grated Parmesan. Cook over low heat until both cheeses have melted and the corn kernels are coated in the mixture. Season to taste, transfer into a heated dish and serve, topped with shredded Parmesan.

VARIATION

A simplified version of this dish is sold at street stalls in Mexico. Whole cooked ears of corn are dipped in cream, then sprinkled with crumbled fresh cheese. Next time you grill, try this as an appetizer. Alternatively, put whole ears of corn in a shallow baking dish and bake them in an oven preheated to 400°F for 30 minutes, until tender and golden. Pour in ½ cup sour cream or crème fraîche, then sprinkle the corn with 2 tablespoons freshly grated Parmesan cheese and serve. The corn can also be brushed with butter and broiled, but it must have plenty of room below the heat, or it will burn.

FRIJOLES DE

TRAVELERS OFTEN SAY THAT "B—— *IT IS TRANSLATED, TASTE DIFFERENT IN MEXICO*
FROM THOSE COOKED ANYWHER—— IS, QUITE LITERALLY, IN THE POT. TRADITIONALLY,
CLAY POTS ARE USED, WHICH G—— ONDERFUL, SLIGHTLY EARTHY FLAVOR. THIS DISH
WOULD BE SERVED AS JUST ONE—— A FORMAL MEXICAN MEAL.

SERVES FOUR

INGREDIENTS

1¼ cups dried pinto beans, soaked
    overnight in water to cover
7½ cups water
2 onions
10 garlic cloves, peeled and
    left whole
small bunch of cilantro
salt

For the toppings
2 fresh red fresno chillies
1 tomato, peeled and chopped
2 scallions, finely chopped
4 tablespoons sour cream
2 ounces feta cheese

COOK'S TIP

In Mexico, the local fresh cheese—*queso
fresco*—would be used as the topping,
but feta makes an acceptable substitute.

se them under
gain. Put the
pan, bring to a

3 While the beans are cooking, prepare
the toppings. Spear the chiles on a
long-handled metal skewer and roast
them over the flame of a gas burner
until the skins blister and darken. Do
not let the flesh burn. Alternatively, dry-
fry them in a griddle until the skins are
scorched. Put the roasted chiles in a
strong plastic bag and tie the top
immediately to keep the steam in. Set
aside for 20 minutes.

4 Remove the chiles from the bag and
peel off the skins. Cut off the stems,
then slit the chiles and scrape out the
seeds. Cut the flesh into thin strips and
put it in a bowl. Spoon all the other
toppings into separate bowls.

5 Ladle about 1 cup of the beans and
liquid into a food processor or blender.
Process into a smooth purée. If you
prefer, simply mash the beans with a
potato masher.

6 Return the bean purée to the pan,
and stir it in. Chop the cilantro,
reserving some leaves to garnish, season
with salt and mix well. Ladle the beans
into warmed individual bowls and take
them to the table with the toppings.

7 Serve the beans with the toppings and
add cilantro to garnish. Traditionally,
each guest spoons a little of the chiles,
tomatoes and scallions over the beans,
then adds a spoonful of sour cream.
The finishing touch is a little feta
cheese, crumbled on each portion.

and add them
le garlic cloves.
on lower the
hours, until the
ere is only a

GREEN RICE

THIS RICE IS RARELY FEATURED ON MENUS IN MEXICAN RESTAURANTS, BUT IS OFTEN MADE IN THE HOME. EXTRA CHILES AND GREEN BELL PEPPER CAN BE DICED AND ADDED AT THE END, IF DESIRED.

SERVES FOUR

INGREDIENTS

2 fresh green chiles, preferably
  poblanos
1 small green bell pepper
1 cup long-grain white rice
1 garlic clove, roughly chopped
large bunch of cilantro
small bunch of fresh flat-leaf parsley
2 cups chicken stock
2 tablespoons vegetable oil
1 small onion, finely chopped
salt

1 Dry roast the chiles and green pepper in a griddle pan, turning them frequently so that the skins blacken but the flesh does not burn. Place them in a strong plastic bag, tie the top securely and set aside for 20 minutes.

2 Put the rice in a heatproof bowl, pour in boiling water to cover and let stand for 20 minutes.

3 Drain the rice, rinse well under cold water and drain again. Remove the chiles and peppers from the bag and peel off the skins. Remove any stems, then slit the vegetables and scrape out the seeds with a sharp knife.

4 Put the roasted vegetables in a food processor, with the garlic. Strip off the leaves from the cilantro and parsley stalks, reserve some for the garnish and add the rest to the processor. Pour in half the chicken stock and process until smooth. Add the rest of the stock and process the purée again.

5 Heat the oil in a saucepan, add the onion and rice and fry for 5 minutes over medium heat until the rice is golden and the onion translucent. Stir in the purée. Lower the heat, cover and cook for 25–30 minutes or until all the liquid is absorbed and the rice is just tender. Add salt and garnish with the reserved herbs. Served with lime wedges, this rice goes extremely well with fish.

YELLOW RICE

THIS RICE DISH OWES ITS STRIKING COLOR AND DISTINCTIVE FLAVOR TO GROUND ACHIOTE SEED, WHICH IS DERIVED FROM ANNATTO.

SERVES SIX

INGREDIENTS

1 cup long-grain white rice
2 tablespoons vegetable oil
1 teaspoon ground achiote seed
  (annatto powder)
1 small onion, finely chopped
2 garlic cloves, crushed
2 cups chicken stock
⅓ cup drained pickled jalapeño chile
  slices, chopped
salt
cilantro leaves, to garnish

COOK'S TIP

Achiote, the seed of the annatto tree, is used as a food coloring and flavoring throughout Latin America. You can buy it at specialty spice shops and ethnic food stores. It is sometimes called annatto powder.

1 Put the rice in a heatproof bowl, pour in boiling water to cover and let stand for 20 minutes. Drain, rinse under cold water and drain again.

2 Heat the oil in a saucepan, add the ground achiote seed (annatto powder) and cook for 2–3 minutes. Add the onion and garlic and cook for another 3–4 minutes or until the onion is translucent. Stir in the rice and cook for 5 minutes.

3 Pour in the stock, mix well and bring to a boil. Lower the heat, cover the pan with a tight-fitting lid and simmer for 25–30 minutes, until all the liquid has been absorbed.

4 Add the chopped jalapeños to the pan and stir to distribute them evenly. Add salt to taste, then spoon into a heated serving dish and garnish with the cilantro leaves. Serve immediately.

CHAYOTES WITH CORN AND CHILES

SHAPED LIKE PEARS OR AVOCADOS, CHAYOTES ARE MEMBERS OF THE SQUASH FAMILY AND HAVE A BLAND TASTE. HOWEVER, THEY GO EXTREMELY WELL WITH OTHER INGREDIENTS, SUCH AS THE CORN AND ROASTED JALAPEÑOS IN THIS MEDLEY.

SERVES SIX

INGREDIENTS

4 fresh jalapeño chiles
3 *chayotes*
oil, for frying
1 red onion, finely chopped
3 garlic cloves, crushed
1⅓ cups corn kernels, thawed
    if frozen
⅔ cup cream cheese
1 teaspoon salt (optional)
⅓ cup freshly grated
    Parmesan cheese

1 Dry-roast the fresh jalapeño chiles in a griddle, turning them frequently so that the skins blacken but do not burn. Place them in a plastic bag, tie the top securely, and set them aside for 20 minutes.

2 Meanwhile, peel the *chayotes*, cut them in half and remove the seed from each of them. Cut the flesh into ½-inch cubes.

COOK'S TIP
Chayotes go by several names, including *christophene* and *choko.* Store them in a plastic bag in the refrigerator and they will keep for up to 1 month.

3 Heat the oil in a frying pan. Add the onion, garlic, *chayote* cubes and corn. Fry over medium heat for 10 minutes, stirring occasionally.

4 Remove the jalapeños from the bag, peel off the skins and remove any stems. Cut them in half, scrape out the seeds, then cut the flesh into strips.

5 Add the chiles and cream cheese to the pan, stirring gently, until the cheese melts. Place in a serving dish.

6 Stir in salt, if needed, then spoon into a warmed dish. Sprinkle with Parmesan cheese and serve. This makes a good accompaniment for cold roast meats.

YOUNG SPINACH LEAVES MAKE
THE ROASTED GARLIC IS AN INS

FROM LETTUCE AND ARE EXCELLENT IN SALADS.
THE DRESSING.

SERVES SIX

INGREDIENTS

1¼ pounds baby spinach leaves
⅓ cup sesame seeds
¼ cup butter
2 tablespoons olive oil
6 shallots, sliced
8 fresh serrano chiles, seeded
  and cut into strips
4 tomatoes, sliced

For the dressing
6 roasted garlic cloves
½ cup white wine vinegar
½ teaspoon ground white pepper
1 bay leaf
½ teaspoon ground allspice
2 tablespoons chopped fresh thyme,
  plus extra sprigs, to garnish

COOK'S TIP
To roast individual garlic cloves simply
place in a roasting tray in a medium
oven for about 15 minutes until soft.

1 M
fror
an chop
and
; pepper,
bay
d thyme in
a jar
se the lid
tight
e dressing
in th
1.

2 Wa
them
towel
g in
j dry
in dish

3 Toast the sesame seeds in a dry frying
pan, shaking frequently over medium
heat until golden. Set aside.

4 Heat the butter and oil in a frying
pan. Sauté the shallots for 4–5 minutes,
until softened, then stir in the chile
strips and fry for 2–3 more minutes.

5 In a large bowl, layer the spinach with
the shallot and chili mixture, and the
tomato slices. Pour on the dressing.
Sprinkle with sesame seeds and serve
garnished with thyme sprigs.

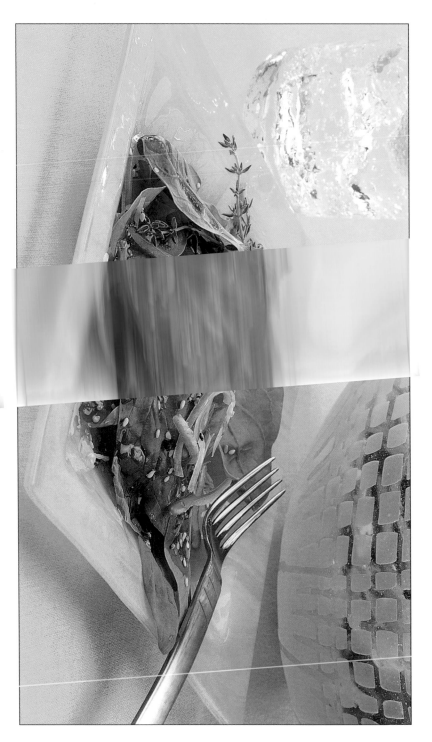

NOPALITOS SALAD

NOPALITOS—STRIPS OF PICKLED CACTUS PADDLES—ARE SOLD IN CANS OR JARS, AND ARE VERY USEFUL FOR MAKING QUICK AND EASY SALADS LIKE THIS ONE.

SERVES FOUR

INGREDIENTS

scant 2 cups drained
 canned *nopalitos*
1 red pepper
2 tablespoons olive oil
2 garlic cloves, sliced
½ red onion, thinly sliced
½ cup cider vinegar
small bunch of cilantro, chopped
salt

1 Preheat the broiler. Put the *nopalitos* in a bowl. Pour in water to cover and set aside for 30 minutes. Drain, replace with fresh water and let soak for another 30 minutes.

2 Place the halves of the red pepper cut side down in a broiler. Broil the peppers until the skins blister and char, then put the pepper halves in a strong plastic bag, tie the top securely to keep the steam in, and set aside for 20 minutes.

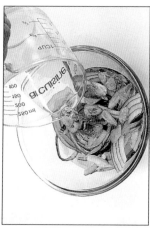

3 Heat the oil in a small frying pan and fry the garlic over low heat until the slices start to turn golden. Using a slotted spoon, transfer them to a salad bowl. Pour the garlic-flavored oil into a pitcher and set it aside to cool.

4 Add the red onion slices to the salad bowl, then pour on the vinegar. Remove the red pepper from the bag, peel off the skins, then cut the flesh into thin strips. Add to the salad bowl.

5 Drain the *nopalitos* thoroughly and add them to the salad, with the cool garlic-flavored oil and a little salt, to taste. Toss lightly, then chill until needed. Sprinkle on the chopped cilantro just before serving. This is delicious served with crusty bread.

JICAMA, CHIL— 1E SALAD

A VERY TASTY, CRISP VEGETABL— —OMETIMES CALLED THE MEXICAN POTATO. UNLIKE POTATO, HOWEVER, IT CAN BE I— AS COOKED. THIS MAKES A GOOD SALAD OR AN APPETIZER TO SERVE WITH DRIN—

SERVES FOUR

INGREDIENTS

1 *jicama*
½ teaspoon salt
2 fresh serrano chiles
2 limes

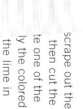

a potato peeler
¾-inch cubes.
/l, add the salt

scrape out the
then cut the
te one of the
ly the colored
the lime in
e.

3 Add the chiles, lime zest and juice to the *jicama* and mix thoroughly to ensure that all the *jicama* cubes are coated. Cut the other lime into wedges.

4 Cover and chill for at least 1 hour before serving with lime wedges. If the salad is to be served as an appetizer with drinks, transfer the *jicama* cubes to little bowls and pass them with toothpicks for spearing.

COOK'S TIP
Look for *jicama* at Asian supermarkets, as it is widely used in Chinese cooking. It goes by several names, and you may find it labelled as either yam bean or Chinese turnip.

CHAYOTE SALAD

COOL AND REFRESHING, THIS SALAD IS IDEAL ON ITS OWN OR WITH FISH OR CHICKEN DISHES. THE SOFT FLESH OF THE CHAYOTES ABSORBS THE FLAVOR OF THE DRESSING BEAUTIFULLY.

SERVES FOUR

INGREDIENTS

2 *chayotes*

2 firm tomatoes

1 small onion, finely chopped

finely sliced strips of fresh red and green chile, to garnish

For the dressing

½ teaspoon Dijon mustard

½ teaspoon ground anise

6 tablespoons white wine vinegar

¼ cup olive oil

salt and ground black pepper

1 Bring a pan of water to a boil. Peel the *chayotes*, cut them in half and remove the seeds. Add them to a boiling water. Lower the heat and simmer for 20 minutes or until the *chayotes* are tender. Drain and set them aside to cool.

2 Meanwhile, peel the tomatoes. Cut a cross in the bottom of each tomato. Place them in a heatproof bowl and pour in boiling water to cover. After 3 minutes, lift the tomatoes out on a slotted spoon and plunge them into a bowl of cold water. Drain. The skins will have begun to peel back from the crosses. Remove the skins completely and cut the tomatoes into wedges.

3 Make the dressing by combining all the ingredients in a screw top jar. Close the lid tightly and shake the jar vigorously.

4 Cut the *chayotes* into wedges and place in a bowl with the tomato and onion. Pour over the dressing and serve garnished with strips of fresh red and green chile.

CAESAR SALA...

ALTHOUGH THIS IS WIDELY REC... ORIGINATED IN MEXICO, AND I... IN HIS RESTAURANT IN TIJUANA... AVOID EATING RAW EGGS.

'CAN CLASSIC, CAESAR SALAD ACTUALLY
1 THE CHEF, CAESAR CARDINI, WHO INVENTED IT
1 WOMEN AND YOUNG CHILDREN ARE ADVISED TO

SERVES FOUR

INGREDIENTS

2 large garlic cloves, peeled and
left whole
¼ cup extra virgin olive oil
4 slices of bread, crusts
removed, cubed
1 Romaine lettuce, separated into
leaves
6 drained canned anchovy fillets
shavings of Parmesan cheese,
to garnish

For the dressing
1 egg
2 teaspoons Dijon mustard
generous dash of Worcestershire
sauce
2 tablespoons lemon juice
2 tablespoons extra virgin olive oil
salt and ground black pepper

1 Cut one garlic clove in half and rub it
around the inside of a salad bowl. Put
the remaining garlic in a large frying
pan. Add the oil and heat gently for
5 minutes, then discard the garlic.
Add the bread cubes to the hot oil, in
batches if necessary, and fry them until
they are crisp on all sides. Drain on
paper towels.

2 Line the salad bowl with the Romaine
leaves. Carefully cut the anchovy
fillets in half lengthwise and distribute
them among the lettuce leaves.
Toss the leaves to spread the flavor of
the anchovies.

3 ...processor
or ...ustard,
W... ...mon juice.
Se... ...d briefly,
th... ...tor running.

4 Pour the dressing onto the salac in
the bowl and toss lightly. Add the garlic
croûtons. Transfer to individual bowls
or carry to the table in the salad bowl.
Sprinkle on Parmesan shavings and serve.

SSERTS

...ngs. Ever since Hernán Cortéz introduced sugar cane
...sserts have been very much on the menu and the array of
...stries in a Mexican pastelería would rival any display
at a European cake shop.

Special cakes and cookies are made for feast days and
festivals, like the Day of the Dead or Twelfth Night.
Kings' Day Bread is traditionally served to celebrate
...piphany, on January 6th, while Mexican Wedding Cookies,
with their generous coating of confectioners' sugar, are a
familiar sight at marriage celebrations.

famous Mexican dessert is Flan, a caramel custard which is
...ar in Spain. Rice puddings of various types are often served,
...ings made from pumpkin or plantains are popular too,
especially with children.

...ver, with the wonderful produce at their disposal, Mexicans
...en opt to end a meal with a simple platter of colorful fresh
fruit, served with salt, chili powder and fresh lime juice,
they did in the days before Spanish and French cooks
introduced them to puddings and pastries.

BUÑUELOS

THESE LOVELY LITTLE PUFFS LOOK LIKE MINIATURE DOUGHNUTS AND TASTE SO GOOD IT IS HARD NOT TO OVER-INDULGE. MAKE THEM FOR BRUNCH, OR SIMPLY SERVE THEM WITH A CUP OF CAFE CON LECHE OR CAFE DE OLLA.

MAKES TWELVE

INGREDIENTS

2 cups all-purpose flour
pinch of salt
1 teaspoon baking powder
½ teaspoon ground anise
½ cup sugar
1 large egg
½ cup milk
¼ cup butter
oil, for deep-frying
2 teaspoons ground cinnamon
cinnamon sticks, to decorate

1 Sift the flour, salt, baking powder and ground anise into a mixing bowl. Add 2 tablespoons of the sugar.

2 Place the egg and milk in a small pitcher and whisk well with a fork. Melt the butter in a small pan.

3 Pour the egg mixture and milk gradually into the flour, stirring constantly, until well blended, then add the melted butter. Mix first with a wooden spoon and then with your hands to make a soft dough.

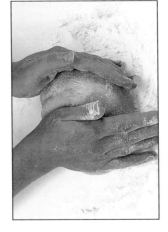

4 Lightly flour a work surface, put the dough on it and knead for about 10 minutes, until smooth.

5 Divide the dough into 12 pieces and roll into balls. Slightly flatten each ball with your hand and then make a hole in the center with the floured handle of a wooden spoon.

6 Heat the oil for deep-frying to a temperature of 375°F, or until a cube of dried bread, added to the oil, floats and then turns a golden color in 30–60 seconds. Fry the *buñuelos* in small batches until they are puffy and golden brown, turning them once or twice during cooking. As soon as they are golden, lift them out of the oil using a slotted spoon and lie them on a double layer of paper towels to drain.

7 Mix the remaining sugar with the ground cinnamon in a small bowl. Add the *buñuelos*, one at a time, while they are still warm, toss them in the mixture until they are lightly coated and either serve immediately or let cool. Decorate with cinnamon sticks.

COOK'S TIP

Buñuelos are sometimes served with syrup for dunking, although they are perfectly delicious without. To make the syrup, mix ¾ cup dark brown sugar and scant 2 cups water in a small saucepan. Add a cinnamon stick and heat, stirring until the sugar has dissolved. Bring to a boil, then lower the heat and simmer for 15 minutes without stirring. Cool slightly before serving with the *buñuelos*.

CAPIROTADA

MEXICAN COOKS BELIEVE IN MAKING GOOD USE OF EVERYTHING AVAILABLE TO THEM. THIS PUDDING WAS INVENTED AS A WAY OF USING UP FOOD BEFORE THE LENTEN FAST, BUT IS NOW EATEN AT OTHER TIMES TOO.

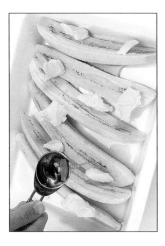

SERVES SIX

INGREDIENTS

1 small loaf French bread, a few
  days old
⅓–½ cup butter, softened, plus extra
  for greasing
scant 1 cup dark brown sugar
1 cinnamon stick, about
  6 inches long
1⅔ cups water
3 tablespoons dry sherry
¾ cup sliced almonds, plus extra,
  to decorate
½ cup raisins
1 cup grated Monterey Jack or
  mild Cheddar cheese
light cream, for pouring

1 Slice the bread into about 30 rounds, each ½ inch thick. Lightly butter on both sides. Cook in batches in a warm frying pan until browned, turning over once. Set the slices aside.

2 Place the sugar, cinnamon stick and water in a saucepan. Heat gently, stirring all the time, until the sugar has dissolved. Bring to a boil, then lower the heat and simmer for 15 minutes without stirring. Remove the cinnamon stick, then stir in the sherry.

3 Preheat the oven to 350°F. Grease an 8-inch square baking dish with butter. Layer the bread rounds, almonds, raisins and cheese in the dish, pour on the syrup, letting it soak into the bread. Bake the pudding for about 30 minutes, until golden brown.

4 Remove from the oven, let stand for 5 minutes, then cut into squares. Serve cold, with cream poured on top and decorated with the extra sliced almonds.

COOK'S TIP
This recipe works well with older bread that is quite dry. If you only have fresh bread, slice it and dry it out for a few minutes in a low oven.

DRUNKEN PLANTAINS

MEXICANS ENJOY THEIR NATIVE FRUITS AND UNTIL THEIR CUISINE WAS INFLUENCED BY THE SPANISH AND THE FRENCH, THEY HAD NO PASTRIES OR CAKES, PREFERRING TO END THEIR MEALS WITH FRUIT, WHICH WAS ABUNDANT. THIS DESSERT IS QUICK AND EASY TO PREPARE, AND TASTES DELICIOUS.

SERVES SIX

INGREDIENTS

3 ripe plantains
¼ cup butter, diced
3 tablespoons rum
grated zest and juice of
  1 small orange
1 teaspoon ground cinnamon
¼ cup dark brown sugar
½ cup whole almonds, in their skins
fresh mint sprigs, to decorate
Crème fraîche or thick heavy cream,
  to serve

1 Preheat the oven to 350°F. Peel the plantains and cut them in half lengthwise. Put the pieces in a shallow baking dish, dot them all over with butter, then spoon on the rum and orange juice.

2 Mix the orange zest, cinnamon and brown sugar in a bowl. Sprinkle the mixture on the plantains.

3 Bake for 25–30 minutes, until the plantains are soft and the sugar has melted into the rum and orange juice to form a sauce.

4 Meanwhile, slice the almonds and dry-fry them in a heavy frying pan until the cut sides are golden. Serve the plantains in individual bowls, with some of the sauce spooned on top. Sprinkle the almonds on top, decorate with the fresh mint sprigs and pass crème fraîche or heavy cream separately.

FRUIT PLATTER

MEXICANS LIKE TO EAT FRUIT WITH CHILE AND LIME AS AN APPETIZER OR HORS D'OEUVRE, BUT THE COMBINATION ALSO MAKES A REFRESHING END TO A MEAL. THE SELECTION OF FRUIT BELOW IS JUST A SUGGESTION; USE ANY FRUIT IN SEASON, BEARING IN MIND THAT THE AIM IS TO PRODUCE A COLORFUL PLATTER WITH PLENTY OF FLAVOR.

SERVES SIX

INGREDIENTS
½ small watermelon
2 mangoes
2 papayas
1 small pineapple
1 fresh coconut
1 jicama
juice of 2 limes, plus lime wedges,
    to serve
sea salt
mild red chili powder

1 Slice the watermelon thinly, then cut each slice into bite-size triangles, removing as many of the seeds as possible. Take a large slice off the pit on either side of each mango, then cross-hatch the mango flesh on each slice. Turn the slices inside out so that the cubes of mango flesh stand proud. Slice these off and put them in a bowl.

2 Cut the payayas in half, scoop out the seeds, then cut each half into wedges, leaving the skin on. Cut the leafy green top off the pineapple, then slice off the base. With a sharp knife, remove the skin, using a spiral action and cutting deeply enough to remove most of the "eyes." Use a small knife to take out any remaining "eyes." Cut the pineapple lengthwise in quarters and remove the core from the center of each piece. Slice each of the pieces into bite-size wedges.

3 Make a hole in two of the "eyes" at the top of the coconut, using a nail and hammer. Pour out the liquid. Tap the coconut with a hammer until it breaks into pieces. Remove the hard outer shell, then use a potato peeler to remove the thin brown layer. Cut the coconut into neat pieces.

4 Peel and slice the jicama. Arrange all the fruits on a platter, sprinkle them with lime juice and serve with lime wedges and small bowls of sea salt and chili powder for sprinkling.

COOK'S TIP
Cut all the fruit into bite-size pieces, so that it can be speared on toothpicks and eaten.

ICE CREAM WITH MEXICAN CHOCOLATE

THIS RICH, CREAMY ICE CREAM HAS A WONDERFULLY COMPLEX FLAVOR, THANKS TO THE CINNAMON AND ALMONDS IN THE MEXICAN CHOCOLATE.

SERVES FOUR

INGREDIENTS
2 large eggs
½ cup sugar
2 bars Mexican chocolate, total
    weight about 4 ounces
1⅔ cups heavy cream
scant 1 cup milk
chocolate curls, to decorate

1 Put the eggs in a bowl and whisk them with an electric beater until they are thick, pale and fluffy. Gradually whisk in the sugar.

2 Melt the chocolate in a heavy saucepan over low heat, then add it to the egg mixture and mix thoroughly. Whisk in the cream, then stir in the milk, a little at a time. Cool the mixture, then chill. Pour the mixture into an ice cream maker and churn until thick.

3 Alternatively, freeze it in a shallow plastic box in the fast-freeze section of the freezer for several hours, until ice crystals have begun to form around the edges. Process to break up the ice crystals, then freeze again. To serve, decorate with chocolate curls.

GARBANZO CAKE

THIS IS A MOIST CAKE, WITH A TEXTURE LIKE THAT OF CHRISTMAS PUDDING. IT IS FLAVORED WITH ORANGE AND CINNAMON AND TASTES WONDERFUL IN THIN SLICES, WITH FRESH MANGO OR PINEAPPLE AND A SPOONFUL OF YOGURT. AS IT CONTAINS NO FLOUR, IT IS A GOOD CHOICE FOR ANYONE ON A WHEAT-FREE DIET.

SERVES SIX

INGREDIENTS

2 x 10-ounce cans chickpeas,
  drained
4 eggs, beaten
1 cup sugar
1 teaspoon baking powder
2 teaspoons ground cinnamon
grated zest and juice of 1 orange
cinnamon sugar (see Cook's Tip),
  for sprinkling

COOK'S TIP

To make the cinnamon sugar, mix ¼ cup sugar with 1 teaspoon ground cinnamon.

1 Preheat the oven to 350°F. Tip the chickpeas in a colander, drain them thoroughly, then rub them between the palms of your hands to loosen and remove the skins. Put the skinned chickpeas in a food processor and process until smooth.

2 Spoon the purée into a bowl and stir in the eggs, sugar, baking powder, cinnamon, orange rind and juice. Grease and line a 1-pound loaf pan.

3 Pour the cake mixture into the loaf pan, level the surface and bake for about 1½ hours or until a skewer inserted into the center comes out clean.

4 Remove the cake from the oven and let stand, in the pan, for about 10 minutes. Remove from the pan, place on a wire rack and sprinkle with the cinnamon sugar. Let cool completely before serving. Try serving this with sliced fresh pineapple.

PECAN CA

THIS CAKE IS AN EXAM
SERVED WITH CAJETA—
USED INSTEAD. TRY SER

INFLUENCE ON MEXICAN COOKING. IT IS TRADITIONALLY
MILK—BUT WHIPPED CREAM OR CRÈME FRAÎCHE CAN BE
H A FEW RED CURRANTS FOR A SPLASH OF COLOR.

SERVES EIGHT TO TEN

INGREDIENTS

1 cup pecans
½ cup butter, softened
½ cup light brown sugar
1 teaspoon vanilla extract
4 large eggs, separated
¾ cup all-purpose flour
pinch of salt
12 whole pecans, to deco
cajeta, whipped cream or
fraîche, to serve

For drizzling
¼ cup butter
scant ½ cup honey

1 Preheat the oven to 350°F
8-inch round spring-form ca
Toast the pecans in a dry fr
5 minutes, shaking frequent
finely into a blender or food
Place in a bowl.

the butter with the sugar in a
wl, then beat in the vanilla
olks.

e flour to the ground nuts and
Whisk the egg whites with the
greasefree bowl until soft peaks
d the whites into the butter
then gently fold in the flour
mixture. Spoon the mixture into
ared cake pan and bake for
es or until a skewer inserted in
or comes out clean.

4 Cool the cake in the pan for 5 minutes,
then remove the sides of the pan. Stand
the cake on a wire rack until cool.

5 Remove the cake from the bottom of
the pan if necessary, then return it to the
rack and arrange the pecans on top.
Transfer to a plate. Melt the butter in a
small pan, add the honey and bring to
a boil, stirring. Lower the heat and
simmer for 3 minutes. Pour onto the
cake. Serve with *cajeta*, whipped cream
or crème fraîche.

Desserts 221

KINGS' DAY BREAD

On Twelfth Night, January 6th, Mexican children receive gifts to mark the day the Three Kings brought gifts to the infant Jesus. This sweetened rich bread, decorated with candied fruit, is an important part of the celebrations. A doll and a bean are hidden inside the cake, and the person who gets the doll has to host a party on February 2nd, another feast day. The person who finds the bean brings the drinks.

SERVES EIGHT

INGREDIENTS

½ cup lukewarm water
6 eggs
2 teaspoons active dry yeast
2½ cups all-purpose flour
½ teaspoon salt
¼ cup sugar
½ cup butter, plus 2 tablespoons
   melted butter, for glazing
1½ cups crystallized fruit and
   candied peel
1½ cups confectioners' sugar, plus
   extra, for dusting
2 tablespoons light cream
crystallized fruit and candied
   cherries, to decorate

1 Pour the water into a small bowl, stir in the dried yeast and set in a warm place until frothy.

2 Crack four of the eggs and divide the yolks and the whites. Place the four yolks in a small bowl and discard the egg whites.

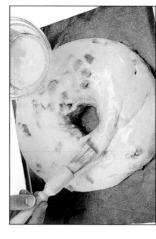

3 Put 1¼ cups of the flour in a mixing bowl. Add the salt and sugar. Break the remaining two eggs into the bowl, then add the four egg yolks.

4 Add ½ cup of the butter to the bowl together with the yeast and water mixture. Combine all the ingredients well.

5 Put the crystallized fruit and peel into a separate bowl. Add ½ cup of the remaining flour and toss the fruit with the flour to coat it.

6 Add the floured fruit to the egg mixture, with the rest of the flour. Mix into a soft, non-sticky dough. Knead the dough on a lightly floured surface for about 10 minutes, until smooth.

7 Shape the dough into a ball. Using the floured handle of a wooden spoon, make a hole in the center, and enlarge.

8 Put the dough ring onto a greased baking sheet and cover lightly with oiled plastioc wrap. Set in a warm place for about 2 hours or until doubled in bulk.

9 Preheat the oven to 350°F. Brush the dough with the melted butter and bake for about 30 minutes or until it has risen well and is cooked through and springy.

10 Mix the confectioners' sugar and cream in a bowl. Drizzle the mixture on the bread when it is cool and decorate it with the crystallized fruit and candied cherries. Dust with confectioners' sugar.

PAN DULCE

THESE "SWEET BREADS" OF VARIOUS SHAPES ARE MADE THROUGHOUT MEXICO, AND ARE EATEN AS A SNACK OR WITH JAM OR MARMALADE FOR BREAKFAST.

MAKES TWELVE

INGREDIENTS

½ cup lukewarm milk
2 teaspoons active dry yeast
4 cups strong all-purpose flour
6 tablespoons sugar
2 tablespoons butter, softened
4 large eggs, beaten
oil, for greasing

For the topping
6 tablespoons butter, softened
½ cup sugar
1 egg yolk
1 teaspoon ground cinnamon
1 cup all-purpose flour

1 Pour the milk into a small bowl, stir in the dried yeast and set in a warm place until frothy.

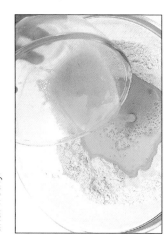

2 Put the flour and sugar in a mixing bowl, add the butter and beaten eggs and mix into a soft, sticky dough.

3 Place the dough on a lightly floured surface and dredge it with more flour. Using floured hands, turn the dough over and over until it is completely covered in a light coating of flour. Cover it with lightly oiled plastic wrap and let rest for 20 minutes.

4 Meanwhile, make the topping. Cream the butter and sugar in a bowl, then mix in the egg yolk, cinnamon and flour. The mixture should have a slightly crumbly texture.

5 Divide the dough into 12 equal pieces and shape each of them into a round. Space well apart on greased baking sheets. Sprinkle the topping onto the breads, dividing it more or less equally among them, then press it lightly into the surface.

6 Set the rolls in a warm place to stand for about 30 minutes, until they are about one-and-a-half times their previous size. Preheat the oven to 400°F and bake the breads for about 15 minutes. Let cool slightly before serving.

ALMOND C

CONFECTIONERS' SUGAI ... INE TO GIVE THESE COOKIES A LIGHT, DELICATE TEXTURE.
THEY CAN BE MADE DA ... ARE DELICIOUS WITH DESSERTS OR COFFEE.

MAKES ABOUT TWENTY-FOUR

INGREDIENTS

1 cup all-purpose flour
1½ cups confectioners' su
pinch of salt
½ cup chopped almonds
½ teaspoon almond extrac
½ cup unsalted butter, so
confectioners' sugar, for
halved almonds, to decora

t the oven to 350°F. Combine
confectioners' sugar, salt and
almonds in a bowl. Add the
xtract.

COOK'S TIPS

Use fancy cutters to make th
look even more interesting. H
crescents are two shapes you
to try.

2 Put the softened butter in the center of the flour mixture and use a knife or your fingertips to draw the dry ingredients into the butter until a dough is formed. Shape the dough into a ball.

3 Place the dough on a lightly floured surface and roll it out to a thickness of about ⅛ inch. Using a 3-inch cookie cutter, cut out about 24 rounds, re-rolling the dough as necessary. Place the rounds on baking sheets, leaving a little space between them. Bake for 25–30 minutes, until pale golden.

4 Let sit for 10 minutes, then transfer to wire racks to cool. Dust thickly with confectioners' sugar before serving, decorated with halved almonds.

MEXICAN WEDDING COOKIES

ALMOST HIDDEN BENEATH THEIR VEIL OF CONFECTIONERS' SUGAR, THESE LITTLE SHORTBREAD COOKIES ARE TRADITIONALLY SERVED AT WEDDINGS, AND ARE ABSOLUTELY DELICIOUS. SERVE THEM AFTER DINNER WITH COFFEE AND PERHAPS A GLASS OF THE MEXICAN COFFEE LIQUEUR—KAHLÚA.

MAKES THIRTY

INGREDIENTS
1 cup butter, softened
1½ cups confectioners' sugar
1 teaspoon vanilla extract
2¾ cups all-purpose flour
pinch of salt
1¼ cups pecans,
    finely chopped

1 Preheat the oven to 375°F. Beat the butter in a large bowl until it is light and fluffy, then beat in 1 cup of the confectioners' sugar, with the vanilla.

2 Gradually add the flour and salt to the creamed mixture until it starts to form a dough. Add the finely chopped pecans with the remaining flour. Knead the dough lightly.

3 Divide the dough into 30 equal pieces and roll them into balls. Space about ¼ inch apart on baking sheets. Press each ball lightly with your thumb to flatten it slightly.

4 Bake the cookies for 10–15 minutes, until they are starting to brown. Cool on the baking sheets for 10 minutes, then transfer to wire racks to cool completely.

5 Put the remaining confectioners' sugar in a bowl. Add a few cookies at a time, shaking them in the confectioners' sugar until they are heavily coated. Serve immediately or store in an airtight pan.

ALMOND ORANGE COOKIES

THE COMBINATION OF LARD AND ALMONDS GIVES THESE COOKIES A GREAT TEXTURE, SO THAT THEY MELT IN YOUR MOUTH. THEY ARE PERFECT WITH COFFEE OR HOT CHOCOLATE.

MAKES THIRTY-SIX

INGREDIENTS
generous 1 cup lard
generous ½ cup sugar
2 eggs, beaten
grated zest and juice of
    1 small orange
1¾ cups all-purpose flour, sifted with
1 teaspoon baking powder
1¾ cups ground almonds

For dusting
½ cup confectioners' sugar
1 teaspoon ground cinnamon

COOK'S TIP

If you can't be bothered to roll out the dough, just divide it into 36 pieces and roll each one into a ball. Place these on baking sheets and flatten each one into a cookie shape with a fork.

1 Preheat the oven to 400°F. Place the lard in a large bowl and beat with an electric beater until light and airy. Gradually beat in the sugar.

2 Continue to whisk the mixture while you add the eggs, orange rind and juice. Whisk for 3–4 more minutes, then stir in the flour mixture and ground almonds to form a dough.

3 Roll out the dough on a lightly floured surface until it is about ½ inch thick. Using cookie cutters, cut out 36 rounds, re-rolling the dough if necessary. Gently lift the rounds onto baking sheets.

4 Bake for about 10 minutes or until the cookies are golden. Let stand on the baking sheets for 10 minutes to cool and firm slightly.

5 Combine the confectioners' sugar and cinnamon. Put the mixture in a small sieve or tea strainer and dust the cookies well. Let cool completely.

FRUIT-FILLED EMPANADAS

IMAGINE BITING THROUGH CRISP BUTTERY PASTRY TO DISCOVER A RICH FRUITY FILLING FLAVORED WITH ORANGES AND CINNAMON. THESE ARE THE STUFF THAT DREAMS ARE MADE OF.

MAKES TWELVE

INGREDIENTS

2½ cups all-purpose flour
2 tablespoons sugar
scant ½ cup chilled butter, cubed
1 egg yolk
ice water (see method)
milk, to glaze
sugar, for sprinkling
whole almonds and orange wedges,
   to serve
For the filling
2 tablespoons butter
3 ripe plantains, peeled and mashed
½ teaspoon ground cloves
1 teaspoon ground cinnamon
1⅓ cups raisins
grated zest and juice of 2 oranges

1 Combine the flour and sugar in a mixing bowl. Rub in the chilled cubes of butter until the mixture resembles fine bread crumbs.

2 Beat the egg yolk and add to the flour mixture. Add ice water to make a smooth dough. Shape it into a ball.

3 Melt the butter for the filling in a saucepan. Add the plantains, cloves and cinnamon and cook over medium heat for 2–3 minutes. Stir in the raisins, with the orange zest and juice. Lower the heat so that the mixture barely simmers. Cook for about 15 minutes, until the raisins are plump and the juice has evaporated. Set the mixture aside to cool.

4 Preheat the oven to 400°F. Roll out the pastry on a lightly floured surface. Cut it into 4-inch rounds. Place the rounds on a baking sheet and spoon on a little of the filling. Dampen the rim of the pastry rounds with water, fold the pastry over the filling and crimp the edges to seal.

5 Brush the empanadas with milk. Bake them, in batches if necessary, for about 15 minutes or until they are golden. Let cool a little, sprinkle with sugar and serve warm, with whole almonds and orange wedges.

COOK'S TIP
Use a little of the leftover egg white instead of milk for glazing, if desired.

CHRISTMA〜ES WITH WALNUTS

MAKES TWENTY-FOUR

INGREDIENTS

½ cup lard
¾ cup confectioners' sugar
1 teaspoon vanilla extract
1 ¼ cups all-purpose flour
¾ cup broken walnuts,
   finely chopped
½ cup confectioners' sugar
2 teaspoons ground cinnamon

〜 oven to 375°F. Place
〜 large bowl and beat
〜ic beater until light

3 Add the flour by hand, working it
gently into the mixture. Do not be
tempted to use a spoon or the mixture
will be too sticky. Add the walnuts and
mix carefully.

4 Divide the dough evenly into 24 small
pieces, roll each to a ball, and space
well apart on baking sheets. Bake for
10–15 minutes, until golden, switching
the baking sheets around halfway
through, to ensure even baking. Cool
the cookies on wire racks.

5 Put the remaining confectioners' sugar
in a bowl and stir in the cinnamon. Add
a few cookies at a time, shaking them in
the confectioners' sugar until they are
heavily coated. Shake off the excess
sugar. Serve wrapped in colored paper.

〜at in ¼ cup of the
sugar, then add
beat well.

COOK'S TIP

Polvo means "dust," and these coo〜
should be crumbly and light to eat
Pecans can be used instead of the
walnuts, if desired

DRINKS

...e great means of slaking thirst, from refreshing fruit drinks ...colate. The traditional drink—pulque—which is made ...ce of the century plant, is very much an acquired taste, but ...ecome popular all over the world, either enjoyed straight, ...ditional way, or as the basis for some wonderful drinks, such as margaritas and bloody Marias.

...rescas, sold at stalls by street traders throughout Mexico, ...ntidote to hot weather. Like licuados and preparados, ...ple and quick to prepare and make a welcome change from the ultra-sweet sodas that are so popular in Europe. A jug of Lime Agua Fresca is the perfect way to welcome guests on a warm summer's evening.

Mexican chocolate typically contains almonds and ...nnamon, two ingredients that are widely used in Mexican ...ooking, and the milky hot chocolate drinks are absolutely ...cious. Corn-based drinks and coffee laced with cinnamon ...enjoyed with meals or served as substitutes for snacks. ...pe, the thick, creamy Mexican eggnog, tastes much more ...n it should, and is a wonderful way to unwind at the end of a stressful day.

TEQUILA

THERE ARE SEVERAL DIFFERENT TYPES OF TEQUILA, MEXICO'S NATIONAL SPIRIT. EACH TYPE OF TEQUILA IS AVAILABLE IN SEVERAL DIFFERENT BRANDS, EACH WITH A DISTINCTIVE FLAVOR INFLUENCED BY THE SOIL TYPE, SUGAR CONTENT OF THE AGAVE PLANTS, CLIMATE, COOKING AND FERMENTING PROCESS.

There are many different ways of serving tequila. Perhaps the best known of these is the slammer, when shots of chilled tequila are drunk with salt and lime. *Joven* (young) or *reposada* (rested) tequila is often served at room temperature in small shot glasses called *caballitos*, and sipped slowly so that all the flavors can be savoured. *Anejo* (aged) tequila should be served in a small balloon glass (a large glass would allow too much of the aroma to escape). It can be diluted with a little water, but ice should not be added.

TEQUILA SLAMMERS

Mexicans have long enjoyed the taste of lime and salt with their food and drink. Beer is also drunk with lime and salt.

INGREDIENTS

chilled tequila
salt
wedges of lime

HOW TO SERVE TEQUILA

Pour a shot glass of tequila. Lick the space between the thumb and the index finger on your left hand, then sprinkle this area with salt. Taking care not to spill the salt, hold a lime wedge in the same hand. Pick up the shot glass in your right hand. Lick the salt, down the tequila in one, suck the lime, then slam down your empty glass. Some drinkers manage salt, lime and tequila in the same hand, but this takes practice.

TEQUILA S

THIS DRINK TAKES ITS ? THE GRENADINE—A BRIGHT RED CORDIAL MADE FROM POMEGRANATE JUICE—F LASS OF ORANGE JUICE AND THEN RISES TO THE SURFACE.

SERVES ONE

INGREDIENTS

1½ tablespoons golden tequ
¼ cup freshly squeezed
   orange juice
juice of 1 lime
1 teaspoon grenadine

cocktail glass with crushed
the tequila, then the orange
ces, which should be freshly
)on't be tempted to use
d orange juice from a carton
ne juice, or the flavor of the
ık will be spoiled.

2 Quickly add the grenadine, pouring it
down the back of a teaspoon held in the
glass so that it sinks to the bottom of
the drink. Serve immediately.

VARIATION
To make a Pink Cadillac, use Gr
Marnier instead of orange juice.

Drinks 233

PINEAPPLE TEQUILA

FLAVORS SUCH AS ALMONDS OR QUINCE HAVE BEEN ADDED TO BLANCO OR REPOSADA TEQUILA FOR SOME TIME. MANY BARS HAVE DEVELOPED UNIQUE FLAVORS BY COMBINING INGREDIENTS SUCH AS CHILES WITH BLANCO TEQUILA AND LETTING THEM SIT FOR A PERIOD OF TIME. THE METHOD BELOW WILL MAKE A SMOOTH FRUITY DRINK.

SERVES SIX

INGREDIENTS

1 large pineapple
2 ounces dark brown sugar
1 litre blanco tequila
1 vanilla bean

1 Rinse a large (about 3½-pint) wide-necked bottle or demijohn and sterilize by placing it in an oven and then turning on the oven and setting it at 225°F. After 20 minutes remove the bottle from the oven with oven mitts and let cool.

2 Cut the top off the pineapple and then cut off the skin, being careful to get rid of all the scales. Cut in half, remove the hard centre core and discard it. Chop the rest of the pineapple into chunks, ensuring that they are small enough to fit in the bottle neck.

3 When the bottle is completely cold, put the pineapple into the bottle. Combine the sugar and tequila in a pitcher until the sugar dissolves and then pour into the bottle. Split the vanilla bean and add it to the rest of the ingredients.

4 Gently agitate the bottle a few times each day to stir the contents. Let the tequila stand for at least 1 week before drinking. When all the tequila has been drunk, the pineapple can be used in desserts such as ice cream or warmed with butter and cinnamon and served with cream.

VARIATION
If desired, add a piece of fresh pineapple and some ice to each glass before serving.

MARGARIT[A]

THE MOST RENOWNED T[...]
MIXED WITH CRUSHED I[...]
THEN POURED INTO THE [...]
[...]HIS CAN BE SERVED OVER ICE CUBES OR "FROZEN" —
[...]HAKER TO CREATE A LIQUID SORBET EFFECT,

SERVES ONE

INGREDIENTS

3 tablespoons tequila
1½ tablespoons triple sec
1½ tablespoons freshly squeezed
  lime juice
crushed ice or ice cubes
lime wedge and salt, for
  frosting glass

[...]il glass by rubbing the
[...]e wedge of lime. Dip
[...]ucer of salt so that it is
[...]is important that there
[...]the glass, so take care
[...]only applied to the

2 Combine the tequila, triple sec and
lime juice in a cocktail shaker, add
crushed ice, if using, and shake to mix.
Carefully pour into the frosted glasses.
If crushed ice is not used, place ice
cubes in the glass and then pour in
the mixture.

COOK'S TIP

White tequila is the traditional spirit
use, but today many people prefer to
make margaritas with reposada tequi[...]
which gives a more rounded flavor.

MANGO AND PEACH MARGARITA

ADDING PURÉED FRUIT TO THE CLASSIC TEQUILA MIXTURE ALTERS THE CONSISTENCY AND MAKES FOR
A GLORIOUS DRINK THAT RESEMBLES A MILKSHAKE BUT PACKS CONSIDERABLY MORE PUNCH.

SERVES FOUR

INGREDIENTS

2 mangoes, peeled and sliced
3 peaches, peeled and sliced
½ cup tequila
¼ cup triple sec
¼ cup freshly squeezed
lime juice
10 ice cubes, crushed, if necessary
(see Cook's Tip)
mango slices, skin on, to decorate

COOK'S TIP
Check that your processor or blender can
be used for crushing ice. If you are not
sure, break ice cubes into smaller pieces
by putting them in a strong plastic bag
and pounding them with a meat mallet.

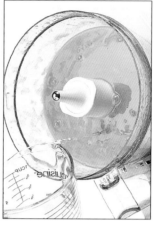

1 Place the mango and peach slices in
a food processor or blender. Process or
blend until all the fruit is finely chopped,
scrape down the sides of the goblet,
then blend again until the purée is
perfectly smooth.

2 Add the tequila, triple sec and lime
juice, process or blend for a few
seconds, then add the ice. Process or
blend again until the drink has the
consistency of a milkshake.

3 Pour into cocktail glasses, decorate
with the mango slices and serve.

LICUADO DE MELÓN

INGREDIENTS
1 watermelon
4 cups chilled water
juice of 2 limes
honey (see method)
ice cubes, to serve

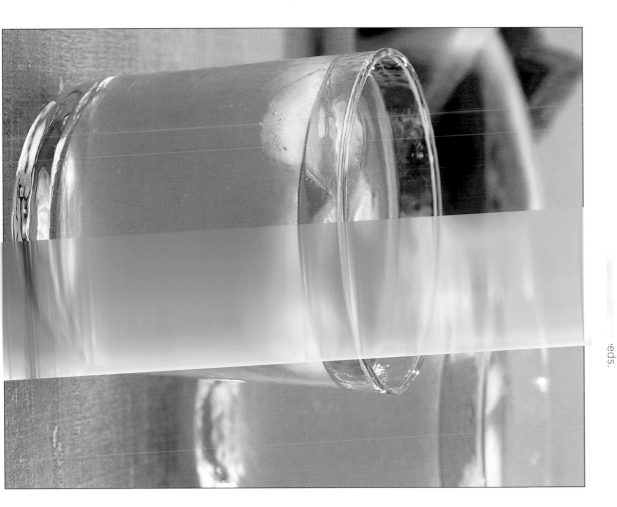

ermelon flesh into chunks,
skin and discarding the
eds.

2 Place the chunks in a large bowl,
pour in the chilled water and let stand
for 10 minutes.

3 Transfer the mixture to a large sieve
set over a bowl. Using a wooden spoon,
press gently on the fruit to extract all
the liquid.

4 Stir in the lime juice and sweeten to
taste with honey.

5 Pour into a pitcher, add ice cubes
and stir. Serve in glasses.

SANGRITA

Sipping sangrita and tequila alternately is a taste sensation not to be missed, the warm flavors of the first balancing the harshness of the second. The drinks are often served with antojitos (nibbles) as an appetizer combo.

SERVES EIGHT

INGREDIENTS

1 pound ripe tomatoes
1 small onion, finely chopped
2 small fresh green fresno chiles,
  seeded and chopped
½ cup juice from freshly
  squeezed oranges
juice of 3 limes
½ teaspoon sugar
pinch of salt
1 small shot glass of golden or aged
  tequila per person

1 Cut a cross in the bottom of each tomato. Place the tomatoes in a heatproof bowl and pour in boiling water to cover. Let sit for 3 minutes.

2 Lift the tomatoes out on a slotted spoon and plunge them into a second bowl of cold water. The skins will have begun to peel back from the crosses. Remove the skins, then cut the tomatoes in half and scoop out the seeds with a teaspoon.

3 Chop the tomato flesh and put in a food processor. Add the onion, chiles, orange juice, lime juice, sugar and salt.

4 Process until all the mixture is very smooth, then pour into a pitcher and chill for at least 1 hour before serving. Offer each drinker a separate shot glass of tequila as well. The drinks are sipped alternately.

COOK'S TIP

This drink can be made with a 14-ounce can of chopped tomatoes and tastes almost as good as when made with fresh tomatoes.

SANGRIA

Testament to the Spanish influence on Mexican cooking, this popular thirst-quencher is often served in large pitchers, with ice and citrus fruit slices floating on top.

SERVES SIX

INGREDIENTS

3 cups dry red wine
juice of 2 limes
½ cup freshly squeezed orange juice
½ cup brandy
¼ cup sugar
1 lime, sliced, to decorate
ice, to serve

VARIATION

In some parts of Mexico a less potent but equally refreshing version of sangria is served. Fill tall glasses with ice. Fill each glass two-thirds full with fresh lime juice diluted with water and sweetened with sugar. Fill up with red wine. Tequila is sometimes added to the lime mixture.

1 Combine the wine, lime juice, orange juice and brandy in a large glass pitcher.

COOK'S TIP

If no sugar is available, use sugar syrup. Heat ¼ cup sugar in ¼ cup water. Boil for 3 minutes, chill and store in a tightly sealed jar.

2 Stir in the sugar until it has dissolved completely.

3 Serve in tall glasses with ice. Decorate each glass with a slice of lime.

CITRUS AGUA FRESCA

THESE REFRESHING FRUIT JUICES ARE SOLD AT STREET STALLS IN TOWNS ALL OVER MEXICO.
THE VARIETIES OF FRUIT USED CHANGE WITH THE SEASONS.

SERVES FOUR

INGREDIENTS

12 limes
3 oranges
2 grapefruit
2½ cups water
6 tablespoons sugar
extra fruit wedges, to decorate
ice cubes, to serve

1 Squeeze the juice from the limes, oranges and grapefruit. Some fruit pulp may collect along with the juice. This should also be used, once any seeds have been discarded. Pour the mixture into a large pitcher.

2 Add the water and sugar and stir until all the sugar has dissolved.

3 Chill for at least 1 hour before serving with ice and fruit wedges. The drink will keep for up to 1 week in a covered container in the refrigerator.

VARIATION
Use pink or ruby red grapefruit instead of white for a slightly sweeter drink with a deeper color.

TAMARIND — RESCA

TAMARIND, SOMETIMES R
SEEDS CAME TO MEXICO
A SWEET-SOUR TASTE ANI

INDIAN DATE, IS NATIVE TO ASIA AND NORTH AFRICA.
ED MEDICINALLY AND AS AN ANTISEPTIC. THE FRUIT HAS
MILAR TO LEMONADE.

SERVES FOUR

INGREDIENTS

4 cups water
8 ounces tamarind pods
2 tablespoons sugar
ice cubes, to serve

ind pulp or paste are sold at
sian food stores. The dried
old in solid blocks. All
s need soaking and sieving,
e spared the time-
k of peeling the pods.

1 Pour the water into a saucepan and heat until warm. Remove from heat and pour into a bowl. Peel the tamarind pods and add the pulp to the warm water. Soak for at least 4 hours.

2 Place a sieve over a clean bowl. Pour the tamarind pulp and water into the sieve, then press the pulp through the sieve with the back of a wooden spoon, leaving the black seeds behind. Discard the seeds.

3 Add the sugar to the tamarind mixture and stir well until dissolved. Pour into a pitcher and chill thoroughly before serving in tumblers filled with ice.

PINEAPPLE AND LIME AGUA FRESCA

THE VIVID COLORS OF THIS FRESH FRUIT DRINK GIVE SOME INDICATION OF ITS WONDERFUL FLAVOR. IT MAKES A DELICIOUS MIDDAY REFRESHER OR PICK-ME-UP AT THE END OF A HARD DAY.

SERVES FOUR

INGREDIENTS

2 pineapples
juice of 2 limes
2 cups still mineral water
¼ cup sugar
ice cubes, to serve

COOK'S TIP
When peeling a pineapple cut off the top and bottom and remove the skin with a spiral action, cutting deeply enough to remove most of the "eyes." Any remaining "eyes" can be cut out using a small knife.

1 Peel the pineapples and chop the flesh, removing the core and "eyes." You should have about 1 pound flesh. Put this in a food processor or blender and add the lime juice and half the mineral water. Purée into a smooth pulp. Stop the machine and scrape the mixture from the side of the goblet once or twice during processing.

2 Place a sieve over a large bowl. Put the pineapple pulp in the sieve and press it through with a wooden spoon. Pour the sieved mixture into a large pitcher, cover and chill in the refrigerator for about 1 hour.

3 Stir in the remaining mineral water and sugar to taste. Serve with ice.

LIME AGUA

THIS IS THE LIME VERSIO... LEMONADE. TRADITIONALLY, LIME PEEL WOULD HAVE BEEN GROUND IN A MOL... THE OIL. MEXICAN LIMES—LIMONES—ARE HARDER AND MORE TART THAN TH... VARIETIES MOST OFTEN SOLD AT WESTERN SUPERMARKETS.

<u>SERVES SIX</u>

INGREDIENTS

7½ cups water
6 tablespoons sugar
10 limes, plus slices, to decor...
ice cubes, to serve

1 Pour the water into a large pitche...
add the sugar and stir until all the...
has dissolved. Chill for at least 1 h...

2 Using a zester or grater, remove th...
zest from the limes, taking care to ta...
only the colored zest, not the pith.
Squeeze the juice from the limes and...
add this to the chilled sugar water, wi...
the lime rind. Stir well and chill again...
until needed. Serve with ice in tall...
glasses, decorated with lime slices.

COOK'S TIP
To extract the maximum amount of juic...
from the limes, roll firmly between your...
palms for a few moments, or pierce wit...
a skewer, put in a bowl, and microwave...
on maximum power for 10–15 seconds...
before juicing. This works with all...
citrus fruits.

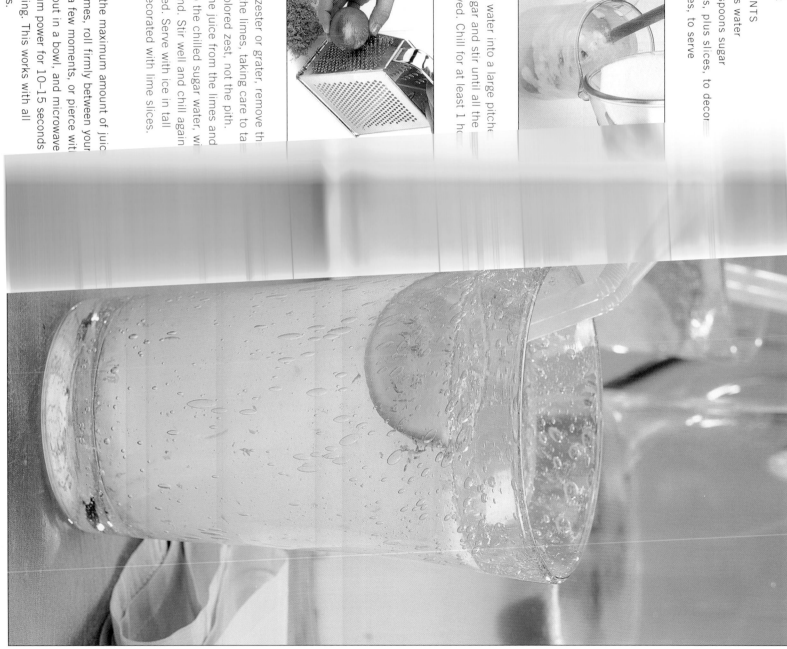

Drinks 243

STRAWBERRY AND BANANA PREPARADO

SIMILAR TO A SMOOTHIE, THIS IS A THICK, CREAMY FRUIT DRINK. LEAVE OUT THE ALCOHOL IF DESIRED.

SERVES FOUR

INGREDIENTS

2 cups strawberries, plus extra, to decorate
2 bananas
4 ounces coconut milk
½ cup water
¾ cup white rum
¼ cup grenadine
10 ice cubes

1 Hull the strawberries and chop them in halves or quarters if they are large fruits. Peel the bananas and chop them into rough chunks.

2 Put the fruit in a food processor or blender, crumble in the coconut and add the water. Process until smooth, scraping down the sides of the goblet as necessary.

3 Add the rum, grenadine, and ice cubes, crushing the ice first unless you have a heavy-duty processor. Blend until smooth and thick. Serve immediately, decorated with the extra strawberries.

BLOODY M

A NATURAL PROGRESSION. . . . .US SIMPLE COCKTAIL CONSISTS OF TEQUILA AND TOMATO
JUICE COMBINED AND SEI. . . . . . . LASS.

INGREDIENTS

1 cup tomato juice, chilled
1 teaspoon Worcestershire sau~
4 tablespoons tequila
few drops of Tabasco sauce
juice of ½ lemon
pinch of celery salt
salt and ground black pepper
ice cubes and 2 celery stalks, ~
into sticks, to serve

led tomato juice into a
nd stir in the tequila. Add
hire sauce and stir the

2 Add a few drops of Tabasco sauce
and the lemon juice. Taste and season
with celery salt, salt and pepper. Serve
over ice cubes, with celery sticks.

CAFE CON LECHE

MANY MEXICANS START THE DAY WITH THIS SPICED MILKY COFFEE, AND THOSE WHO HAVE ENJOYED A HEARTY MIDDAY MEAL WILL OFTEN OPT FOR A CUP OF IT WITH A PASTRY AS THE AFTERNOON MERIENDA.

SERVES FOUR

INGREDIENTS

⅔ cup ground coffee
2 cups boiling water
2 cups milk
4 cinnamon sticks, each about
   4 inches long
sugar, to taste

1 Put the ground coffee in a cafetière or pitcher, pour on the boiling water and let sit for a few minutes until the coffee grounds settle at the bottom.

2 Push down the plunger of the cafetière or strain the pitcher of coffee to separate the liquid from the grounds. Pour the strained coffee into a clean pitcher.

3 Pour the milk into a heavy pan, add the cinnamon sticks and bring to a boil, stirring occasionally.

4 Using a slotted spoon, lift out the cinnamon sticks and use a smaller spoon to press down on them to release any liquid they have absorbed. Set the cinnamon sticks aside for serving.

5 Add the coffee to the hot milk, then pour into cups. Add a cinnamon stick to each cup. Drinkers should add sugar to taste as needed.

HORCHATA

THIS DELICIOUS, AROMATIC RICE DRINK TASTES WONDERFULLY CREAMY, YET DOES NOT CONTAIN A DROP OF MILK. MEXICANS SWEAR BY IT AS A MEANS OF SETTLING UPSET STOMACHS OR CURING HANGOVERS, AND IT IS OFTEN SERVED AT BREAKFAST.

SERVES FOUR

INGREDIENTS

2¼ cups long-grain rice
3 cups water
1¼ cups blanched whole almonds
2 teaspoons ground cinnamon
finely grated zest of 1 lime, plus
   strips of zest, to decorate
¼ cup sugar
ice cubes, to serve

1 Put the rice in a sieve and rinse thoroughly under cold running water. Drain, transfer to a large bowl and pour in the water. Cover and soak for at least 2 hours, preferably overnight.

2 Drain the rice, reserving 2½ cups of the soaking liquid. Spoon the rice into a food processor or blender and grind as finely as possible.

3 Add the almonds to the processor or blender and continue to grind in the same way until finely ground.

4 Add the cinnamon, grated lime zest and sugar to the ground rice and ground almonds. Add the reserved soaking water from the rice and mix until all the sugar has dissolved.

5 Serve in tall glasses with ice cubes. Decorate with strips of lime rind.

CAFE DE OLLA

This is one of the most popular drinks in Mexico. The name means "out of the pot," which refers to the container in which the coffee is made. Traditionally, the sweetener is piloncillo, the local unrefined brown sugar, but any dark brown sugar can be used. This coffee is always drunk black.

<u>SERVES FOUR</u>

INGREDIENTS

4 cups water
½ cup *piloncillo* or dark brown sugar
4 cinnamon sticks, each about
  6 inches long
⅔ cup freshly ground coffee, from
  dark-roast coffee beans

COOK'S TIP

If you do not have a fine sieve, improvise with a regular sieve lined with coffee filter paper. For a special occasion serve the coffee with chocolate-dipped cinnamon sticks, which can be used to stir with.

1 Place the water, sugar and cinnamon sticks in a saucepan. Heat gently, stirring occasionally to make sure that the sugar dissolves, then bring to a boil. Boil rapidly for about 20 minutes, until the syrup has reduced by a quarter.

2 Add the ground coffee to the syrup and stir well, then bring the liquid back to the boil. Remove from the heat, cover the pan and let stand for around 5 minutes.

3 Strain the coffee through a fine sieve, pour into cups and serve immediately.

ATOLE

This drink, which is made from white corn masa, is traditionally flavored with piloncillo (Mexican unrefined brown sugar) and ground cinnamon. It has the consistency of a thick milkshake. Fresh fruit purées are often added before serving, and some recipes introduce ground almonds or milk.

<u>SERVES SIX</u>

INGREDIENTS

1¾ cups white *masa harina*
5 cups water
1 vanilla bean
¼ cup *piloncillo* or dark
  brown sugar
½ teaspoon ground cinnamon
1 cup fresh strawberries, chopped
  pineapple or orange segments
  (optional)

1 Put the *masa harina* in a heavy saucepan and gradually beat in the water to make a smooth paste.

2 Place the pan over medium heat and add the vanilla bean and bring the mixture to a boil, stirring constantly until it thickens. Beat in the sugar and ground cinnamon and continue to beat until the sugar has dissolved. Remove from heat.

3 If adding the fruit, purée it in a food processor or blender until smooth, then press the purée through a sieve.

4 Stir the purée into the corn mixture and return to the heat until warmed through. Remove the vanilla bean. Serve.

AFTER-DINNER COFFEE

A SUPERB END TO A MEAL. KAHLÚA, THE MEXICAN COFFEE LIQUEUR USED IN THIS DRINK, IS ALSO DELICIOUS SERVED IN A LIQUEUR GLASS AND TOPPED WITH A THIN LAYER OF CREAM.

SERVES FOUR

INGREDIENTS

⅓ cup dark-roast ground coffee

2 cups boiling water

½ cup tequila

½ cup Kahlúa liqueur

1 teaspoon vanilla extract

2 tablespoons dark brown sugar

⅔ cup heavy cream

1 Put the ground coffee in a heatproof pitcher or cafetière, pour on the boiling water and let sit until the coffee grounds settle at the bottom.

2 Strain the coffee through a sieve or push down the plunger in the lid of the cafetière to separate the liquid from the grounds. Pour the strained coffee into a clean heatproof pitcher.

3 Add the tequila, Kahlúa and vanilla to the coffee and stir well to mix. Add the sugar and continue to stir until it has dissolved completely.

4 Pour the mixture into small coffee cups, liqueur coffee glasses or tall glasses that will withstand the heat of the coffee.

5 Hold a teaspoon just above the surface of one of the coffees. Pour the cream very slowly down the back of the spoon so that it forms a pool on top of the coffee. Repeat with the remaining coffees. Serve immediately.

VARIATIONS

If you prefer, you can use Tia Maria instead of Kahlúa, or even a chocolate liqueur.

ROMPOPE

LEGEND HAS IT THAT IL
PUEBLA. SOME VERSIONS
SUCH AS RASPBERRIES. I1
OR STRIPPED EARS OF CO
S FIRST MADE IN THE KITCHENS OF A CONVENT IN
'H GROUND ALMONDS OR SERVED WITH FRESH BERRIES
SEAL BOTTLES OF ROMPOPE *WITH ROLLED CORN HUSKS*

MAKES 6¼ CUPS

INGREDIENTS

4 cups milk
1½ cups sugar
½ teaspoon baking soda
1 cinnamon stick, about 6 inch
12 large egg yolks
1¼ cups dark rum

1 Pour the milk into a saucepan and s
in the sugar and baking soda. Add the
cinnamon stick. Place the pan over
medium heat and bring the mixture to
a boil, stirring constantly. Immediately
pour the mixture into a bowl and cool
to room temperature. Remove the
cinnamon stick, squeezing it gently to
release any liquid.

2 Put the egg yolks in a heatproof bowl
over a pan of simmering water and
whisk until the mixture is very thick
and pale.

3 Add the whisked yolks to the milk
mixture a little at a time, beating after
each addition.

...ture to a clean pan,
...at and cook until the
...and the back of the
...hen a finger is drawn

5 Stir in the rum, pour into sterilized
bottles and seal tightly with stoppers or
plastic wrap. Chill until needed. Serve
rompope very cold. It will keep for up
to 1 week in the refrigerator.

CHAMPURRADA

THIS POPULAR VERSION OF ATOLE IS MADE WITH MEXICAN CHOCOLATE. A SPECIAL WOODEN WHISK CALLED A MOLINOLLO IS TRADITIONALLY USED WHEN MAKING THIS FROTHY DRINK.

SERVES SIX

INGREDIENTS

4 ounces Mexican chocolate, about
    2 discs
5 cups water or milk, or a mixture
7 ounces white *masa harina*
2 tablespoons dark brown sugar

COOK'S TIP

If you can't find Mexican chocolate, improvise by mixing 4 ounces dark bitter chocolate (minimum 70 percent cocoa solids) with ¼ cup ground almonds, ¼ cup sugar and 2 teaspoons ground cinnamon in a food processor. Process until a fine powder is obtained.

1 Put the chocolate in a mortar and grind with a pestle until it becomes a fine powder. Alternatively, grind the chocolate in a food processor.

2 Put the liquid in a heavy saucepan and gradually stir in all the *masa harina* until a smooth paste is formed. Use a traditional wooden *molinollo*, if you have one, or a wire whisk for a frothier drink.

3 Place the pan over medium heat and bring the mixture to a boil, stirring constantly until the frothy drink thickens.

4 Stir in the ground chocolate, then add the sugar. Serve immediately.

MEXICAN HOT CHOCOLATE

MEXICAN CHOCOLATE IS FLAVORED WITH ALMONDS, CINNAMON AND VANILLA, AND IS SWEETENED WITH SUGAR. ALL THE INGREDIENTS ARE CRUSHED TOGETHER IN A SPECIAL MORTAR, AND HEATED OVER COALS. THE POWDERED MIXTURE IS THEN SHAPED INTO DISKS. MAKING THE CHOCOLATE IS DIFFICULT BUT FORTUNATELY THE DISKS CAN BE BOUGHT AT SPECIALTY STORES.

SERVES FOUR

INGREDIENTS

4 cups milk
2–4 ounces Mexican chocolate
    (1–2 disks)
1 vanilla bean

VARIATION

If you prefer, you can use dark bitter chocolate instead of Mexican chocolate. You will need slightly less, as the flavor will be more intense.

1 Pour the milk into a saucepan and add the chocolate. Precisely how much to use will depend on personal taste. Start with one disk and use more next time if necessary.

2 Split the vanilla bean lengthwise using a sharp knife, and add it to the milk.

3 Heat the chocolate milk gently, stirring until all the chocolate has dissolved, then whisking with a wire whisk or a *molinollo* until the mixture boils. Remove the vanilla bean and divide the drink among four mugs or heatproof glasses. Serve immediately.

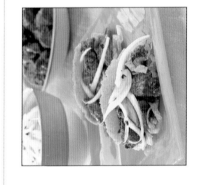